DARE TO JUMP

CEDRIC DUMONT

DARE TO JUMP

EVERYTHING YOU WANT IS ON THE OTHER SIDE OF FEAR

« **Cover: Pyramids of Giza**

It took six years of negotiations with the Egyptian Government and Air Force to be granted permission for two flights above the pyramid complex. This was a world first and was achieved thanks to our strong team on site. Great teamwork made success possible.

This book was originally published as *Dare to jump*.
Je droomleven begint buiten je comfortzone, LannooCampus, 2020.

D/2020/45/191 – NUR 800
ISBN 978 94 014 6896 1

COVER DESIGN	Peer De Maeyer
PAGE DESIGN	Keppie & Keppie
COVER PHOTO	Noah Bahnson
TRANSLATION	Lynn Butler

LannooCampus Publishers is a subsidiary of Lannoo Publishers, the book and multimedia division of Lannoo Publishers nv.

LannooCampus Publishers
Vaartkom 41 bus 01.02
3000 Leuven
Belgium
WWW.LANNOOCAMPUS.COM

Postbus 23202
1100 DS Amsterdam
Netherlands

TABLE OF CONTENTS

My very first base jump with my friend and mentor Thierry Van Roy. The jump took place in Saint Vith, from a bridge of 70 metres high along the highway – ideal for a first jump.

It was early morning. I stood 70 metres above the ground on a bridge in Saint Vith, Belgium.

There was not a breath of wind. The sky was grey. There was still some fog in the valley.

Next to me stood my good friend and mentor Thierry Van Roy, perfect company.

I was ready for it.

Ready for my very first base jump.

For over two years, I had prepared myself mentally for this moment. Ever since I started skydiving, I knew that base jumping would be the end goal.

I felt no special pressure to jump. I didn't have to do it and I had no expectations of what it would be like.

That morning in Saint Vith I just felt that jumping was possible.

I had packed my parachute myself just as Thierry had taught me.

Thierry is gone now. Barely five years later, Thierry would fail over an outcrop of rocks in the Swiss mountains.

But I wasn't thinking about the future, that morning on the bridge.
All that mattered to me was the moment itself.

70 metres was not so high and I had faith in myself and in Thierry.

The desire was bigger than the fear.

I was so focused, so completely absorbed by the process, that I didn't pay attention to the environment or to the landscape. I didn't notice the trees or hear the birds.

At a certain moment I let everything go.

I bent my knees slightly.

I pulled back my arms.

I jumped.

Less than half a minute later, I was on the ground. I was euphoric.

I had taken an unbelievably big step and had confirmed something.

The moment that I had thought about for so long had finally arrived and I knew: I can do this!

This photo was taken at a base jump from an antenna near Brussels, a spot where we went every weekend to jump. It was easily accessible and the perfect place for gaining experience. Today, there are cameras everywhere – times are changing ...

FOREWORD

I have a lot to share.

Sometimes it seems that I have so much to say that I can't decide where to start. But don't worry: I will get straight to the point, because my first priority is to be helpful.

I have always been fascinated by high performance. Why do some people take more risks and why are they better at dealing with uncertainty or fear? Many people freeze when the pressure becomes too great, or they panic and make the wrong decisions. But some people perform better under pressure. What makes us behave so differently?

I have read a lot of books about leadership and performance. I learned that most of them are quite similar and often so long-winded that their tips become lost. So most of the time they just sit on the shelf. That is unfortunate.

That will not happen with this book.

What I will tell you is not nuclear physics. My recommendations on how to improve your performance involve three basic principles. You may have already heard of or read about them. However, principles can be difficult to apply in real life.

'You know the path, but you're not walking it.'

We are going to do something about this. *Dare to Jump* is based on my experiences. It presents the best of the tips and techniques that I find most useful, the ones that I use every day. I have learned what works and what doesn't. This book will be like a pocket knife: helpful in many situations.

I've always wondered: how do you become the best version of yourself? Why is it that some people manage to follow their own path and, something extremely important, how do they achieve satisfaction and fulfilment?

There is a very strong link between performance and happiness. Happiness needs to lie at the centre of everything with our achievements orbiting it.

The opposite will not work. If you define yourself by only your performance, titles and achievements, at one point you will become unhappy.

When I take a good look at myself, I can see that everything starts in my head. This means that when I write about high performance, I have to write about thoughts and emotions. Our lives and specifically how we experience our lives, result from how we think, feel and respond to what happens to us. How do our thoughts and emotions determine the choices we make and the course of our lives? The question that fascinates me particularly is: how do we create the lives we dream of?

My point is this: since the way you think determines who you are and who you will become, increasing your awareness of your thoughts and emotions will increase your power to realise your potential. This is how to become the person you want to be, or the person you actually are. This is how you empower yourself.

Self-awareness is the starting point for establishing a positive relationship between performance and satisfaction. Many people perform because they have to, because they are afraid of losing their job, because they need money, or because they have been taught that they must do their best always and everywhere. For me, performing well relates to feeling that I am following my own path and making my dreams come true. It is an emerging process, and not a reaction. Self-awareness is key!

The question is:

Do you know yourself?

The even bigger question is:

Are you brave enough to be yourself?

Why are you performing?

Where do you get satisfaction?

What do you want to do with your life?

It's worth repeating that if you want to drive your performance in a positive way, you have to get to know yourself. You have to know your strengths and your weaknesses and where you want to go. This is *self-leadership*. You can't lead anyone else if you can't lead yourself. If you know yourself, you will be much stronger as a person and you will be able to tackle your fears.

This book will help you to overcome your fear and give you three *power skills* to help you become the best version of yourself. They are: a limitless mindset, a laser focus and the trust edge.

These are not imaginary skills. They are the real skills that I use in an environment where complacency and a lack of focus lead to death.

This book is not meant to encourage you to put yourself in danger. Instead, it shows you that taking calculated and educated risks is the only option if you want to grow as a person and as a leader. *To fly you have to dare to jump.*

1

FROM FEAR TO FLOW

'Fear is the mind-killer. Fear is the little-death
that brings total obliteration. I will face my fear.'

— Frank Herbert, *Dune* —

WHY I DO WHAT I DO

I was not particularly mentally strong when I was a child. I was very sensitive and I still am, although I have learned to keep this in check. Actually, these days I can come over as rather insensitive and behave like a huge control freak.

I was always very curious and inquisitive. I devoured books and had a library full of information about aeroplanes and dangerous animals. I was never interested in dogs. I would have rather had a poisonous black mamba or red-back spider.

My parents gave me every opportunity to try and do things without forcing me. If I really got hooked, I could continue with it. But what I had to do, was to show them that I was driven.

When I was three years old, I stood on skis for the first time. Skiing was my first sport. When I was four, I started skateboarding. My father had brought a skateboard from California and I immediately learned to slalom skate with it.

I was a rather good student, good enough that I could occasionally stay away from school for a few days to travel with my father on business trips, which is how I started playing golf at the age of nine. My father brought me with him to a business meeting at a Floridian resort where there was a golf club. The manager of the pro-shop gave me a club and a golf ball and said, "Here you are, go hit this around for a bit." I had never heard of golf, but I liked it. As a kid, I found it very challenging.

I played competitive golf until I was nineteen. At one point I realised that I was not good enough to be a professional golfer, to be playing on the tours. But I learned a lot from golf, like how to make good choices and sacrifices, cultivating discipline, focus and dedication.

As a teenager I became as disciplined as a professional golfer. While my friends were playing, I was training and hitting balls. My parents would say, "Go outside and play with your friends." I would reply "No, I have to wash my clubs before the tournament and get enough sleep." Even then I saw myself as a nomad. I didn't want to get stuck in or work in any one place. A desire for freedom appeared at a very young age. Joining in my father's business trips had exposed me to an appealing lifestyle revolving around golfing, skiing and surfing, being good at something and travelling a lot. I ended up with that lifestyle, but in a completely different industry.

"Someday I will fly," I said when I was seven years old. At school I told people that I was from another planet and would one day fly away from the playground. My teacher said, "Flying? People can't do that." That was a harsh statement, but she did not kill my dream. I thought: we'll see about that later. She did not realise that what she had said only encouraged me more.

It was clear to me from a young age that if I wanted to make my dreams come true and achieve something, I had to focus on them. Even then I refused to be held back by other people's rules, by obligations that you supposedly have to follow in order to live a good life but that actually lock you in chains.

Is studying and getting a diploma unimportant? No. Knowledge is power, but both are not everything. They provide no certainty of a job, a house, or a family, if that is what a person is looking for. I had two options: I could do what people expected of me or I could do what I really wanted to do.

You do not have to follow the set rules. Life can be different. Nevertheless, I entered university to study law. In parallel, I founded a company. After three years of study, I realised that I would not complete my degree. I did not see myself as a lawyer. Working in a law firm was not my dream. That was my starting point, the moment when it became clear that the choice was up to me. I was ready to live my own life, independent of my parents.

As a twenty-year-old I found a way to buy a Range Rover with a crazy idea. How did I do it? It was my father's idea. He suggested that I sell advertisements on my, not yet purchased, Range Rover. I thought it was impossible and yet I gave it a try. I picked up the phone and called around my network: "Hello, I have a fantastic offer for you." I asked for 50,000 Belgian francs or €1250 per advertisement.

One day I met with a Brussels caterer and spent sixty minutes trying to convince him to take up my offer only for him to conclude: "I am not interested in buying such a tiny advertisement." "Okay. Sorry," I said and got up to leave. He responded, "No, wait! How much for an advert on the roof of your car? Everyone who is on a floor above ground level will see your roof." I swallowed and said, "300,000 Belgian francs," which was about €7500, and the deal was done.

After landing fifteen customers, I was able to buy my car. The Range Rover dealer was very enthusiastic and my car appeared at all possible events. I ended up with an annual turnover of 4 million Belgian francs or about €100,000.

I think that I was a good salesman and entrepreneur. I would not become a lawyer and the Range Rover project was a success, but my dream was to become a pilot. Flying and an adventurous life was becoming my top focus.

I travelled to the United States. I have been a fan of that country since I first travelled there with my father on his business trips. California in particular appealed to me. It's the mecca of technological innovation and of action sports culture. You can surf, skate, skydive, climb, cycle, you name it and I like the energetic, creative mentality of the US, particularly California.

I ended up in Oceanside in southern California, a small surf city on the Pacific Ocean, and headed for a local airport. There was a pilot school to the left of the runway. Clean-cut people walked around, wearing crisp shirts and smart suits. On the other side of the runway was a skydive centre. The people there had tattoos and punk hairstyles. Two worlds came together at that airport, just like they came together in me, because I was into flying and adventurous activities. I stood on the runway asking myself if I would become a pilot or skydiver. Should I turn left or right?

Pilots must adhere to a long list of rules. This leaves a very small margin in which to taste freedom. Skydiving had a much stronger association with freedom for me. It was more exciting than sitting in a machine, following procedures and filling in papers. I tried to imagine my life as a pilot with a major airline. Did I see myself doing that? No.

I turned right and headed for the skydiving school. Its environment appealed to me the most. Alternative, exclusive and very minimalist. With skydiving there is not much hassle: you pull a small parachute pack around your shoulders and you are gone. I liked its simplicity and the ability to move quickly.

Skydiving was for me a summary of everything I wanted: flying, minimalism and risk taking. It was gliding on air, like a surfboard glides on water. It combined freedom and travel with the discipline and focus that I had learned from golf and, like surfing and skateboarding, it was an outdoor activity. I continued to develop new businesses but skydiving became my focus.

After my success with the Range Rover, I founded an agency that organised events. I made a good living from it and, more importantly, the business allowed me to travel and to skydive five months a year. I worked in Belgium and travelled to California and Florida every winter to jump. For me, that balance has always been crucial. I ran the agency for seven years and then sold it for a good price. I was financially comfortable and could invest in new projects.

Many people adjust their consumption patterns to their income level but I never spend much money on luxuries. I try to save because I believe that my success might not continue, that it is just too good to last. The idea that my current business could be my last golden egg is in the back of my mind. Yet, uncertainty in business makes business exciting for me. I wonder what the next year will bring. Maybe I am simply lucky, but my success is also a result of good timing. I meet the right people at the right time.

I am more of an entrepreneur than a top athlete, although I never plan to set up a large company. My definition of being an entrepreneur means that I can organise my job around my life, not the other way around.

I prefer to call myself an adventurepreneur. I lead an exciting life full of adventure. Freedom remains my guideline and yet I am building something. I have never had a wage or a boss because I have created all my jobs myself. I am good at creating jobs that can be perfectly combined with my passions.

And base jumping is my passion, far more than a hobby. In the beginning I did not earn any money from it. That was never my intent. But becoming a base jumper and earning money from my passion for sport was yet to come.

"Don't do it," said a bearded man. "It's too dangerous."

I was in a skydiving club in Florida and had just told the bearded man that I wanted to get into base jumping. His answer made my urge to try it even greater. I knew that base jumping was what I had to do.

When I was six years old, I went with my father on a business trip to New York City. He had an appointment at the Windows on the World restaurant, on the top floor of the north tower of the World Trade Center. The restaurant had a ties-only dress code. My father did not wear ties so he had to wear one from the restaurant. But what I remember best were the floor to ceiling windows that gave the restaurant its name. I remember thinking, "Could I fly away from here?" Not could I jump, but could I fly? I think it was the emptiness that attracted me. When I saw images of base jumpers, years later, I knew that I had found it. Base jumping was flying like a bird. It was the ultimate freedom.

Base jumping requires even more engagement than skydiving. When you jump from an aeroplane you carry a main parachute and a reserve. The lower heights of base jumps mean that you only have time to open one parachute so a backup makes no sense. Also, base jumping is often illegal.

On the other hand, although base jumping is higher risk than skydiving, the procedure and equipment requirements and the overall hassles of base jumping are less than for skydiving. You don't need a plane, you don't have to set up a major logistics operation. You just need yourself, a high object and a parachute. Minimum input leads to maximum output. The return from base jumping in terms of emotions and satisfaction is exponentially greater than from skydiving. Nothing has brought me closer to my dream of flying and feeling alive than base jumping.

People sometimes ask me: "Why do you do that?" Yes, why do I jump from buildings? That is like asking a climber why he is venturing up Mount Everest, knowing that one in ten climbers does not return alive. My answer is, "To get to know myself. To go to the deepest parts of myself and to push my limits. To know how far I can go as a human being."

<blockquote>
'If you don't confront your fears, you will never get to know your deepest self.'
</blockquote>

Remember the movie Point Break, with Patrick Swayze and Keanu Reeves? Swayze's character, Bodhi, is the leader of a group of Californian surfers and bankrobbers. If they are not on the water or waving guns around, they go skydiving. One of Bodhi's lines is: *'If you want the ultimate rush, you've got to be willing to pay the ultimate price.'* That goes for me too, when I base jump. I experience the ultimate rush and at the same time I accept that I can die. To feel freedom, you have to accept uncertainty. Freedom lies in being bold.

Patrick de Gayardon died on 13 April 1998. Patrick was one of the pioneers of the wingsuit, a suit that lets you fly through the air. It was a wingsuit crash that killed him.

A year later I crawled into a wingsuit myself.
　　Patrick inspired me. I had met him and had seen pictures of him, and I knew: the wingsuit would be my next thing. His death didn't change that.
　　I built my first wingsuit with a friend. We were among the first people to make them. A lot of progress has been made since then. Our suit was a prototype, but I am still here. My aim was not to perform spectacular stunts. My greatest dream remained the same as always: to fly like a bird.
　　Many base jumpers had accidents in that period because people made wrong decisions or misjudged situations and hit the cliff or the tower from which they jumped. A wingsuit allows you to fly away from the cliff and open your parachute when you are far enough from it.

My first and only jump off a cliff in Belgium. This is "Le rocher de Freyr", a well-known place for climbers. With a launch point only 55 metres above ground this is not a high jump, but the surroundings are so breathtaking that it is definitely worth it. This jump was also a first in Belgium.

Skysurfing was my first real competitive discipline in the late 1990s. I came from a surf-
and-skate environment, so I wanted to fly with some kind of snowboard on my feet.

After a while I started to find it boring. That is why we invented proximity
flying. We stayed as close as possible to a rock, we skimmed past it. Only a few
other people tried it, precisely because it was so dangerous. But it made my
dream come true: I flew like a bird.

"What are you up to these days?" asked the marketing manager of Red Bull.
"I've seen your name pop up in the news from time to time." I was at a party in
Brussels. It was early 2000, one year after my events agency was sold to a large
group. I replied that I flew to every corner of the world to jump as a wingsuit
pilot, skysurfer or base jumper.

 The man nodded and said that Red Bull was looking for extreme sports
athletes to sponsor and invited me to visit Red Bull's Austrian headquarters.
I agreed. The trip to Austria was a fantastic experience. I met for one week
with the Red Bull people to find out if I matched the brand. Red Bull athletes
don't only have to be very good at their sport, they also have to have the right
personality and be creative. We clicked.

Becoming a Red Bull athlete was a fresh start and the timing was perfect. For the next ten years I did nothing but travel and jump. One day Christopher Reindl, a senior Red Bull Media executive, asked me if I would give a talk to Red Bull Basement University members about dealing with fear. This was a surprise. "Sure, no problem," I replied and thought, "Speak? Me? To a group of people? Impossible!"

Another speaking invitation arrived at the same time from Vincent Herbert, the former CEO of Le Pain Quotidien. He asked me to speak at the headquarters of his bakery chain. He had conquered the world from Brussels and had just moved his headquarters to New York. Despite all my expectations, people responded very enthusiastically to my talks. Red Bull even encouraged me to do more of them. This is how I became a speaker for corporate organisations and the like and began mentoring athletes and business people to perform at their peak level. I had finally found the perfect combination of my sport, my history and who I was as a person and began to travel the world telling my story and inspiring people.

Although my life and career have been full of variety and change, my ideas and values have been consistent. Public speaking is also a form of minimalism, I need no more than the ideas in my head to spread the word with a strong purpose.

What is important to me is that my story and perspectives can help other people who want to change their lives but do not know where to start. I want to give people wings, so they can fly too. I did not plan all of this. I just believe that it's up to me to write my life story.

Mentoring elite athletes and entrepreneurs has given my life a new dimension and I can do it without compromising my freedom. It has taught me a lot. One of the people I mentor is Sergio Herman, one of the greatest chefs in the world. It is amazing how that man inspires me with his passion, creativity and dedication.

When I started mentoring people in leadership positions, I also began a one-year study of high performance psychology. I wanted to frame why some people performed well but others reached much, much higher levels of performance. As ever, this topic remained a fascination. I explained earlier that I was not mentally strong as a child. It was through sport that I became mentally strong. My studies allowed me to explain in concrete terms how I was able to go the extra mile, how I could perform better under pressure and how to better deal with emotions like fear or stress.

'I believe that the seduction of complacency
and an easy life is one hundred times more brutal,
ultimately, than a life where you go all in and take
an unconquerable stand for your highest dreams.'

— Robin Sharma —

My studies also got me thinking. I had read many books about *flow hacking* and *energy management*. The result of this work is the three *power skills* that I want to share with you: a rocket mindset, a laser focus and trust.

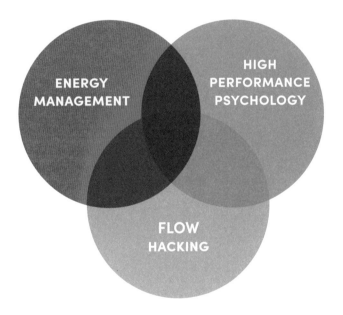

As a skysurfer I participated twice in the famous X-Games.
Since 2000 I have focused entirely on wingsuits and base jumping.

The experience of public speaking was the perfect way for me to reinvent myself and remain credible and relevant. After all, every new generation of action athletes takes far more risks than the previous one, and as time passed my desire to take risks diminished. Many of my colleagues and friends lost their lives practising extreme sports. My son was born in 2012, which brought me much happiness. But I have always found that happiness can make you weak. You become less of a warrior, you no longer throw yourself so whole-heartedly into new extreme adventures – because you have so much more to lose!

I kept on flying, because it is still my greatest passion and drive. But over the years, my passion for public speaking and for making an impact on people has only grown. This led to the idea of writing a book in which I would tell my story. Writing a book is also an emotional risk. As you can see, I took the leap.

Self-awareness is a form of emotional intelligence. It is being aware of what you do and say, what you think and, most importantly, what you feel. Self-awareness is the first step to high performance and satisfaction.

> 'The number one thing that differentiates good and great? Self-awareness!'

As I mentioned before, self-awareness is key. You should always ask yourself the question: do I know myself? But an even bigger question is whether you are brave enough to be yourself. That last part is the most important.

I did what was right for me, but please do not repeat what I have done. It is possible that my choices would make you very unhappy. You have to do what you want to do.

> 'Leadership starts with self-awareness.
> Learn about yourself first before you think
> about leading others.'

Self-awareness is the difference between good and great. We may think we know ourselves, but that is usually not the case. Our thoughts and actions run largely on automatic pilot. This is not necessarily a bad thing. Our habits, behaviour, routines and impulses can carry us through life without having to stop and think about our actions. Our brain does not need our consciousness to go to the toilet, drive a car or have a drink. Without our automatic pilots, we would forget how to drink and every car ride would become a very tough mental task because every action would have to be conscious. Our auto-pilots take a lot of work off our hands. Unfortunately, sometimes we forget that we are on auto-pilot. When we are not sufficiently aware of our emotions and thoughts, they begin to control us subconsiously. As a result, we become slaves to the mechanisms of our brains and worse we become addicted to this.

That is not what we want.

Fortunately there is a remedy to break this addiction. It consists of five steps.

1. Moderate your opinions

—————

'Be less opinionated.'

It is not necessary to have an opinion about everything. You can make yourself unhappy by always having to judge everything, by always thinking about how the world should be rather than seeing it for what it is. Accept things as they are, it's the healthiest approach.

2. Take yourself less seriously

—————

'Lighten up.'

Yes, you too are replaceable. The world is not about you, there are almost 8 billion other people on this planet. So do not take yourself too seriously and do not take life too seriously. Nothing lasts forever, including us.

3. Discover your patterns of thinking

—————

'Learn your bullshit patterns.'

A lack of self-awareness can lead people to make the same mistakes over and over again. For example, let's say that you have a relationship and after five years it gets in the way. You actually realised from the beginning that you weren't right for each other. So you end the relationship but only days later you fall for a very similar person. You haven't learned from your mistakes.

It is very common for people to not recognise their behaviour patterns, in their private lives and at work. Suppose someone changes jobs because communication with their colleagues is difficult. They join another company thinking that their problem will be solved because they will have new colleagues. But they run into the same problem because they were the one with a communication problem. Changing jobs, work and environment was easier than facing their problem.

4. Recognise the problems that you create yourself

'You attract what you are.'

We all know people who seem to be constantly running into problems. Either they imagine problems where none exist or they make bad choices that cause their problems. Consider, for example, people who cannot moderate their alcohol consumption. They drink too much during a dinner, they get drunk, but they still drive. And then they get involved in an accident. "I was unlucky," they say. The truth is that they made a bad choice for the umpteenth time. They could have chosen to drink less, or not at all, or chosen not to drive.

Some people perpetually insist that their setbacks are the result of circumstances or the behaviour of others. If you have problems you have to dare to ask yourself: "What could I have done to avoid this problem? Can I make better choices in the future?" This means being fully accountable. It means owning your actions. Too many people don't take ownership of their lives, even if it's all they want. The majority of us live our lives as victims. The moment you accept total responsibility for everything in your life, is the day you claim the power to change anything in your life.

5. Be realistic

'If you look for bad, you get bad.'

Seeing ourselves and the world in a realistic way is not easy. There is often a big gap between our identity and our reputation, between how we see ourselves and how others see us. Our thoughts define us, often much more than we realise. You attract what you radiate. Anyone looking through negative glasses will attract misery. Why? Because you lose your ability to redirect your life in a positive direction. If you do not believe that something will succeed, it won't because you won't make an effort to succeed.

Fortunately, the opposite is also true. The more positive your perspective is, the more attractive you will be to positive people. More opportunites will come your way and you will be more open to taking them. Better self-awareness will lead to better choices and this leads to better results and ultimately to more satisfaction and fulfilment.

Preventing automatic responses from controlling you is important, but don't overlook that negative thoughts and emotions can keep you in chains. Negativity can have a much greater influence on what we do than you might suspect.

There is a link between thoughts and actions. A thought very often becomes an action. All our small, daily actions become habits and habits give direction to our lives. So, the more positive your thoughts are, the greater the chance that your actions, your habits and ultimately your life will become strong and positive.

That sounds obvious, but there is one problem: our brains appear to be primarily programmed for negative thoughts and emotions. We owe this to the fight-or-flight response, an instinct that can overwhelm us. This is logical, because responding to fear can be necessary for survival. If our ancestors had not felt fear when a large predator suddenly appeared, they would have been gobbled up before they could reproduce.

That response is still in us, even though a constant fight for survivial is not a common feature in western society. But non-life-threatening situations also stoke up adrenaline and other stress hormones. For example, from the moment your boss shouts at you to come into their office, your blood pressure begins to rise and your heart starts pounding. Your body is already bracing itself.

When we feel stress or fear of failure, we begin to focus on what can go wrong. You approach your boss's desk, knees shaking, expecting a scolding. Did you perhaps do something wrong? Will you be fired? You do not know why your boss is angry, but you are already trying to figure out how to defend yourself. We were not programmed with the fight-or-flight response to deal with situations like this, but it can still be our default response and we cannot simply switch it off.

Transformation and change, two similar but different phenomena, can also induce negative thoughts. The fear of change is ingrained in people. In times of change, most people automatically think about what can go wrong. But we can also think: could change improve things and create new opportunities?

Discarding negative emotions is difficult. They stick to our brains like velcro, while positive emotions slip away as if coated in Teflon. How can you deal with this? Is there a cure? Yes. Self-awareness. The more aware you become of your habits and wishes, the more you discover something frightening.

'We are full of shit.'

A large percentage of our thoughts, arguments and actions are just reflections of what we feel at a certain moment. We feel something and do something, but don't think about it. These are nonsense thoughts that get us started. It is only when we are very aware of what we feel and why, that we can convert negative emotions into positive ones. Without insight into ourselves, it is not possible to fill our brains with positive thoughts.

Unfortunately, there is no switch in our head that allows us to switch on our self-awareness. We have to work on it. It is a process of developing awareness on three levels: our distractions, our reason for existence and our blind spots.

1. What distracts you?

'What the hell are you doing?'

What captures your attention? It is OK to have distractions. We need them because sometimes it is important to just clear your mind. At night, for example, sometimes I watch Netflix. It might not be high quality viewing, but it can calm my mind. My thoughts are taken to another part of the world, far away from the day's concerns and that is great.

A caveat: nowadays we live in a world full of distractions. There are simply too many distractions and we are constantly being drawn to them, for example, by social media. This can make you want to do everything and want to be everywhere. Before you know it, these distractions have wasted time that could have been spent on the things you really wanted to do. So, you need to be very selective about what things and projects you let distract you. You must choose them; they must not choose you. This is about shifting from Fear of Missing Out (FOMO) to Joy Of Missing Out (JOMO).

2. Why do you do what you do?

'What the hell are you feeling?'

Most people do not dare to ask themselves fundamental questions. Questions like: Am I who I think I am? Do I do what I really want to do? Or, do I do what people expect me to do? Most people glide over the surface of life. They follow outdated social or cultural rules that no longer apply.

A very well-known rule is that you must study so that you can get a degree and a good job. I am not saying that studying is a bad thing, if you know what you want to achieve by studying. Many people study because they think that is what is expected of them. They regard a degree as a form of security. If you do not study, you will not have money and without money you cannot join the consumer society.

What is the alternative?

I do not advocate that you just drop everything and go live in a forest, unless that is what you really want to do. It's important that you ask yourself how you feel and that you discover how you really are. Instead of just doing what you are told to do, it is important that you get to know yourself and discover how you react to things in your life. What gives you satisfaction and what does not?

The Japanese have a wonderful theory about this. They believe there are four important reasons to do something: you love to do it, you are good at it, you can make money doing it, and the world needs it. Where those four points converge is your sweet spot, called your *Ikigai* in Japan. If you find your *Ikigai* you can make better choices. But to find it you must get to know yourself.

3. Where are your blind spots?

'What the hell are you not seeing?'

We all have our *blind spots*, also called areas for development. Knowing your strengths is important because you must use them and develop them. But you must know your blind spots too, so that you know what you are not good at and what you must avoid. If you want to avoid crossing your own limits, you need to know where your limits are today, so you can work on expanding them later. The place to start is to find your blind spots and work on them.

'My biggest strength is my ability, every day,
to recognise my weaknesses.'

— Satya Nadella, CEO Microsoft —

Very few people dare to question themselves. This is logical because it causes feelings of doubt and insecurity. For some people it is easier to blame others than to ask themselves if they have acted too emotionally or communicated poorly.

Take the case of a woman leaving her husband for another man. Many men might react by thinking, "I'm going to kill that man for taking my wife." Was it really the other man's fault or did he make his wife so unhappy that she could not stand it anymore and left him?

Blind spots are often the result of self-limiting beliefs. This happens when your assumptions limit your options. This happens to me too. Sometimes, for example, I do not dare to dream big enough. Restrictive patterns of thinking, like that, are less of a problem than they used to be. But I remember the first time I had to give a presentation to a large group of people at a big company. I kept on thinking that I just wasn't ready for it. Of course, I was ready, I was just afraid of failing.

Another blind spot of mine is that I can sometimes be very lazy, and I used to procrastinate. If I had to do something, I would always wait until the last minute to do it. Since I know that laziness and procrastination are problems, I can work on them. However, with time, I believe we procrastinate because something is not a priority, or we just lack motivation or purpose.

My communication skills are also sometimes a weak point. Sometimes I think people have understood me perfectly, but then they feed interpretations back to me that are all wrong. That means that I have not been clear enough. Since I know this is a problem, I pay attention to it.

We must dare to recognise our blind spots. This means that self-awareness can only help us if we can accept ourselves. We do ourselves no favours when we sweep our blind spots under the carpet.

If you know who you are, what you can and cannot be, what you feel and where you want to go, you have already taken a very important first step towards knowing yourself. But you are not there yet. Now it is time to get down to work.

When I give presentations on this topic, people often say, "Cedric, you haven't said anything about hard work, training and perseverance!" That is correct. Why do I not do that? Well, my answer is always the same: "Because hard work is a basic, a given, it is something you have to do and I cannot offer you any tricks to get around the need for hard work."

Achievements are often a matter of choices and hard work is simply a part of that. You will need to invest time and energy and get fully engaged. For people who are passionate about what they do or have a clear purpose, this will be so obvious that I do not need to mention it.

A warning: If you perform just for the sake of it and not out of purpose and passion the outcome is almost never good.

'Have big goals – but don't tie your happiness to your goals. You must be happy before you attain them.'

Performing in the absence of self-awareness can be very bad.

There is something known as the *Performance Paradox*. It describes situations where the harder that people work, the less satisfaction they get from their work. This phenomenon occurs when work is not a passion but an obsession. When you perform for the sake of performing and not because your work satisfies you, you become frustrated. So, you perform even more because your feelings of frustration and your inability to feel satisfied leads you to think that you are just not good enough at what you do.

Base jump from the Artevelde Tower in Ghent, with a height of 118.5 metres. The jump took place with the permission of project developer Ignace De Paepe, just before he sold the building to KBC.

This is the fastest road to burnout. You may be in the best job you have ever had, but if you are always under stress, feeling overwhelmed and always forcing yourself to keep up the pace out of fear of losing your job, you will inevitably burnout at some point.

People who burnout are often perfectionists. They put themselves under enormous pressure to the point that they lose their resilience. Instead of attaining satisfaction from their work, it drains them of all their energy.

That is the dark side of performance and achievement.

> 'We all climb a ladder, but make sure the ladder
> is on the right side of the wall.'

Believe it or not, sometimes building a career can be at your own expense.

A desire to climb up the career ladder can be motivating. But the drive that pushes you up the ladder can lead you away from jobs that you found satisfying. Some intrapreneurs and entrepreneurs are so fixated on performing that they forget what is essential in life. They climb ever upwards at the expense of their health, their family life and their bonds with their children. Constant striving to achieve puts them under so much pressure that they lose sight of what is important in life. That is why I always ask people who are obsessed with their careers: "Who will be at your bedside when you die, your family or your colleagues?"

> 'Destroy the idea that you have to be constantly working
> or grinding in order to be successful. Embrace the concept
> that rest, recovery and reflection are essential parts
> of the progress towards a successful and happy life.'

If you are always achievement-oriented, you will constantly live in the future. You will become addicted to results. Once you achieve your target, you are already looking ahead to the next one. As a result, you forget to enjoy the here and now.

This is a conundrum that is not easy to solve, because you simply enjoy doing your job, so it is extremely difficult to say no and draw a boundary. But if you do not, it is inevitable that you will eventually become terribly disheartened and the job that you once thought of as the opportunity of a lifetime will no longer give you any satisfaction whatsoever.

Performance that is primarily ego-driven is often done at the expense of other people. We have all met entrepreneurs who are so driven by money, power and status that they seem ready to step on other people to get it. They may be successful and able to buy whatever they want. But something is missing in their heart: satisfaction. Fulfilment.

I have also come across many entrepreneurs who started their companies with enormous passion. Their companies grew and they built a team around them. Their companies began to make a profit, but somehow, they lose touch with the reason they started it in the first place. This phenomenon is known as the Growth Paradox: Growing is good, but does it have to continue for ever? Are there no limits?

One of my friends is an entrepreneur who fell into the Growth Paradox trap. He started small, but he was an incredible salesman. His greatest happiness was meeting people and winning them over. The only thing is that now he sits at his desk all day behind his computer. He misses the freedom and contact with people that he once had as well as the excitement of selling. His company sales have increased ten-fold over the last ten years, but he gets zero satisfaction from it. Sure, your business can grow, but it should not grow at the expense of your happiness and throw your life off-balance.

Believe me, I know from speaking to many famous people who seem to lead the perfect life that you can read about in the paper that they no longer get satisfaction from what they do. They may be successful, but their success does not necessarily make them happy.

I have heard the same song so many times, "You are so lucky with your work and your life, but me, I'm stuck."

Oh. Is that right? I am lucky, am I?

Or could it be that I made different choices than you did, that I did not always do what was expected of me? Maybe I just dared to accept uncertainty.

When I started, I did not have a single euro. But I had other valuable resources. I was full of drive, curiosity and optimism. I had a strong belief in my abilities and vision.

I remain very grateful to my parents for letting me be who I was and allowing me to follow my own path. Thanks to them, I am motivated by something besides performing just to perform, achievement for achievement's sake. The education they gave me is priceless. I want to pass that on to my son because it was the most beautiful gift that they could have given me. My parents gave me a toolbox that opens any door. I hope that my son will also dare to question everything.

Sometimes I meet people who I believe have done better than me. I learned to ask myself: "How can I also get there or become as good?" That is, only if I wanted to be in their place. I never undertook a new challenge out of envy. In fact, until I reached the age of 12, I had never encountered that emotion.

When I first realised that some people envied what others had or were doing, it was hard for me to understand their mentality. I remember thinking, "Wow, it is possible that some people really are envious?"

When I was growing up, we never compared our family to other families and we only rarely judged what other people did. We were brought up to believe that constantly comparing yourself to others makes you deeply unhappy. You can shout, "Hey, he has more potatoes than me!" Well, maybe he does, but do you really want more potatoes? If you do, then you better do something about it because they are not going to fall from the sky onto your plate.

'Stop wishing, start doing.'

Performing is an activity. It involves doing something, whether it is kneading bread, guiding people on a walk, or writing a book. But you need to look at performing in a broader context. After all, what we do is related to what we feel, who we are and what we dream about.

People are searching, more and more, for a different performance model than the one that has been the norm for decades. It is becoming clear that continually increasing the quality of your performance leads to nothing if it provides you with no satisfaction. Therefore, I like to talk about Performance 2.0.

What does that mean, Performance 2.0?

It begins with being yourself. If you want to perform to the max, you must be able to choose to be yourself! You need to create the space to be vulnerable, because vulnerability can be very inspiring. The way you perform and what you do when you perform should also be fully aligned with your core values, since it is your core values that define who you are as a human being.

Performing in a healthy way means that you follow your own path, but you do it empathetically. This applies absolutely to leaders, if you want to keep your team in good form – particularly in times of disruption and transformation. This is because many people cite a lack of empathy in their leader as the reason that they changed jobs. Interpersonal emotional intelligence is required to keep your team feeling positively motivated. As a leader, you need to be able to put yourself in their place and demonstrate that you can see things from the team's perspective. Never think that you can boost performance by scaring your team. Fear kills productivity.

'I've never been frightened of failure,
only of failing to give my best.'

— Gary Player —

Fear.

I can talk about it for hours. Because of what I do, I must talk about it.

I am often asked: "Don't you get scared?" A lot of people think that those of us who take big risks with high consequences do not feel fear. They think that people involved in extreme activities suffer from some sort of mental disorder that makes them fearless. They think of us as some sort of mutants with supernatural powers.

The idea that those involved in extreme disciplines are special is a myth that I always try to disprove. For example, sometimes I meet people who want to fly like I do. They are often eager to point out that they are fearless. I always respond to this by saying, "The day that I stop feeling fear is the day that I stop jumping. If you don't feel fear, you become stupid! Unconscious and very stupid!"

A person who is not scared is much less conscious of their actions and so they do stupid things more quickly than others. The chances of someone like that becoming old are small.

I consider myself to be a very normal person. I do not believe that I have a deviant brain. So sure, I feel fear like everyone else. Emotions have functions. In high-risk environments, fear has a clear function. Fear makes me aware that I am doing something dangerous, that I am taking risks that have high consequences!

So, what is the difference between me and people who avoid taking risks?

It has to do with how a person deals with emotions and fear in particular. Many people will not dare to take on anything that they are afraid of. They are, effectively, disabled by what I call *negative* fear. Through experience and training it is possible to turn negative fear into *positive* fear. I use positive fear to deal in a conscious way with myself and my environment. This takes a high level of self-awareness. You need to know your limits, how much fear you can manage, and you must be certain that you are making good decisions.

Dealing with your fear is a tool to help you be realistic about risk, its dangers and its consequences. You need to be able to rationalise your response to fear. You can learn to use fear as a motivator to give you a boost.

If you can do this, fear will become your friend.

Most people know fear as the fear of failure or rejection, or the fear of not being able to control a situation in our life. This means that they do not dare to follow their own path and realise their full potential. They get stuck in a life they do not like because they are afraid to take the plunge into what really excites them.

Many parents raise their children through fear. When their child is faced with the slightest risk the parent warns, "Don't do that, it's dangerous!" As a teenager, if you do something that is out of line you are told, "Umm, that's a bit risky. Do you really want to do that?" You reach twenty and your once big dreams have been diminished to, "Ooof, I'm not sure if I dare to do that." This is the culture of fear in which many of us are raised.

Fear is the oldest human emotion. Our primary reaction to fear is the fight-or-flight response. Without that mechanism you see no danger and you run straight into your own danger.

> 'Being scared is part of being alive.
> Accept it and walk through it.'

So, fear is essential for our survival. But, equally, it is a very unpleasant emotion. Despite having spent more than twenty years in a high-risk environment and after having clocked up more than 13,000 jumps, that annoying emotion still raises its head. So, why do I keep taking risks?

The answer is simple: I take calculated risks to confront and overcome my fear. That is exactly what makes it so exciting. You do not let your fear control you. You take control of your fears and you use fear to your best advantage.

Overcoming my fear makes me feel alive. That makes me happy and fulfilled.

The starting point for daring to do something is not the point where you no longer feel fear. When you have the courage to overcome your fear, you are ready to be bold. A person who has overcome their fears will have developed a strong sense of self-awareness and become the architect of their own life. This is how you generate the power to become who you want to be and make your dreams come true.

When you control fear you empower your life.

> 'Someone who controls fear, generates
> the power to become whom he wants.'

How do you overcome your fears? People often ask me, "What's the trick?"

Sorry, there is no trick, there are no shortcuts. There is only a strategy. Overcoming fear is hard work.

Your brain is not a muscle, but like a muscle it can be trained and developed to change the way you think about and respond to internal and external stimuli. This is referred to as neuroplasticity. Given enough mental discipline and repetition, we can literally change the routes that thoughts take as they travel through our minds to cause a response. Confronting your fears can, in this sense, be like a mental workout. The more you do things outside of your comfort zone, the faster you learn to respond differently to these things and turn negative fear into positive fear. This takes quite some effort, but the more you repeat it, the more physiologically and emotionally straightforward it will be and your courage to change and undertake things will increase in parallel.

> 'Leave your comfort zone. Step into the unknown.
> The rest, you'll find while doing it.'
>
> — Mike Horn —

Doing something that scares you every day will help you to grow as a person. You will discover and expand your potential as well as your limits. You will come in touch with your deepest self and begin to perform better and achieve more.

Overcoming your fear is done in three steps.

1. Accept fear!

> 'Become the observer.'

By simply accepting fear, you will change your perception of it. Anxiety and stress are very normal emotions. Even though they can be unpleasant, and perhaps because they are, they serve a purpose. Accepting that emotions are something you must deal with puts you in the position of an observer rather than a victim.

I often say, "Deal with it, fear is part of your life." Do not dramatise your fear. It is okay to be anxious and to feel stressed sometimes.

We have a choice. Publishing a book can scare me because I can be criticised, but I still choose to do it. Just as I choose to jump from buildings. In the end, we always have a choice: we can choose to do something or to not do it.

If I do not do something, I may no longer feel fear, but I may feel regret.

I may feel sorry that I did not take a risk because I know that without taking risks, I will not make the progress I wish to make in my life.

An emotion is a moment, regret is permanent.

2. Give up on control

When I am about to jump off a mountain or a building, there are certain factors I can fully control, such as my equipment and myself. However, there are many factors, such as the weather, over which I have zero control. If I were not able to put that thought aside, I would never jump.

If you are constantly compelled to control everything, in the long run you will not control anything. This may seem to be a paradox, but it is true. By being willing to be in control all the time, your thoughts and attention will be focused on the future. You will increase your anxiety or fear of failure. This will cause you to lose control over the here and now. All that will be achieved is that you will become restless and distracted. The result, usually, is that we take no action at all because our thought processes have made us unsure about the outcome. So ultimately, the need to control everything leads to performance anxiety. You do not dare to start anything because you do not know how it will end.

Many people are afraid of failure and of what others will say or do if they fail to achieve their goal. This insecurity restricts them, and as a result, they underperform. This can lead to a culture of fear of failure in their workplace.

My view is the opposite: if I am certain about the outcome of something, I find it boring. Certainty makes me fall asleep. To me, it is about immersing myself in the now, being fully engaged in the action and most importantly, believing in what I do.

'The more I immerse myself in the present moment, the more I know something good is going to happen in the future.'

Many high achievers fear that if they try something new, things could go wrong. They are wary. This does not have to be a problem. Recognising and accepting uncertainty keeps you sharp and focused. It forces you to reinvent yourself. This is not a reflection on a person's confidence. It is a sensible response to uncertainty.

Is there anything you can do about that? No.

Do you have to reinvent yourself to stay relevant? Yes. That encourages you to be innovative, creative and sharply focused on your goal.

Accepting uncertainty and discomfort is the best decision I have ever made in my life, it makes me feel alive.

'Most people want certainty.
They will not act on their dreams because their dreams
don't have a certain outcome.'

Most people prefer external security over inner freedom. But if you have inner freedom, you will be fully capable of embracing the uncertainty that is a part of chasing your dreams. The more you accept this reality, the more relaxed you will be. You will know, at the core of your being, that if you want something, you will go and get it.

If you hang on to your dreams and follow the process of developing yourself into someone who can achieve your goals, then nothing is impossible.

My recommendation is that you need to stay focused and not chase after everything. Match your goals to your self-awareness, meaning be aware of your capabilities, your potential and your limitations and strive to become the person who can achieve your goals.

3. Trust yourself

Most of us behave as if we are confident. However, that does not seem to be the case. This is due to fear of failure. Fear of failure destroys self-confidence. The lower your performance anxiety, the higher your self-confidence. Someone who has absolutely no fear of failure will project a lot of self-confidence.

A trick to combat performance anxiety is:

'Having no expectations.'

We always have expectations about how things should be. But if you can let go of expectations, you will achieve real freedom.

That is the subtle art of not giving a fuck.

I say that very clearly in my presentations: "I have made choices in life based on what I need. I need to manage my expectations not yours. So, I don't care what you think."

'Have the courage to be disliked.'

That concept is called the detachment of outcome. It means that you distance yourself from a certain result. Expectations block people. This is how expectations can destroy us.

For example, if you visit a customer, full of expectations and desperate to get the outcome or the deal that you have envisioned, you put a lot of unnecessary pressure on yourself. You burden yourself with performance anxiety. If you have no expectations, you will reduce your anxiety, this will create a more relaxed atmosphere and increase your chances of establishing a rapport with the customer.

The same thing can happen in a job interview. If you enter the interview with the idea in your mind that not being offered the job will constitute a failure and rejections, you will increase your anxiety, this will erode your self-confidence and you will not perform well.

You strike a deal; you get the job? Great!

No deal? No job offer? No problem. You have not lost anything, and you have grown your network and learned something.

Managing my expectations is not easy. I have learned to be more detached and to have no expectations. I expose myself to new situations and people and I see what happens.

I even accept that I can die.

I really have no problem with that idea. For the sake of clarity, that does not mean that I do not care about my life, but that I accept the consequences of what I do. If you accept that something can fail, you give yourself a lot of self-confidence. You will not be paralysed by fear of failure, you will take action and this will increase the chance that something will succeed.

I am often asked, "Are you conscious of the fact that you can die doing what you do?"

"But that applies to you as well," I always answer. "Sitting still is ultimately deadly."

Many people are not afraid of death, but of life. I am very afraid of death, but not at all afraid of living.

Man likes to live in denial. We do not want to think about the end because that is hard. The problem is that we are not always aware of the fact that our days are numbered. Our presence on Earth is very limited. Life is like a roll of toilet paper: the more you approach the end, the faster it rolls away.

Your time is your most precious asset. Do something with it.

Becoming aware of your own mortality will shelter you from fear. Becoming aware of my mortality helps me to maintain my relationship with time. When you realise that you may have only twenty more summers, and if you want to get as much out of your life, as much experience, as possible, a tremendous amount of urgency is created and the fear decreases.

Another first was our base jump of the Avaz Tower in Sarajevo (176m).
This licensed jump was a first in Sarajevo.

The late Steve Jobs captured my sentiments perfectly:

> 'Remembering that you are going to die
> is the best way I know to avoid the trap
> of thinking you have something to lose.'

Indeed! We have nothing to lose at all. Staying in touch with your mortality is an incredibly strong way to convince yourself to act. In a hundred years we will not be here anymore and no one will care about what you did or didn't do.

In past centuries it was a custom to carry a small object or to wear a piece of jewellery, a *memento mori*, to remind the bearer of their mortality. This still applies. We need to keep in mind that this has not changed.

Cedric Dumont, a famous adventurer, entrepreneur and author, once commented:

> 'Don't take life too seriously,
> because no-one comes out alive.'

No matter what you do in your life, you will die. That is a liberating thought. Once you realise that your time is very limited, you become much more aware that your life is not a rehearsal, but the real thing.

> 'You have one shot!'

If you are going to do something, now is the time. This is the reason why you need to make a conscious decision to live the life that you want, not someone else's.

> 'You have to build your own life résumé.'

When you are caught up in routine, time passes very quickly. You stop enjoying what you do, and you cannot become enthusiastic about what you could be doing instead. All those seconds, minutes, hours and days spent in that routine are gone forever. In the end, you could throw away months and even years this way.

It is not a pleasant thought, but you need to face the facts. You only have a limited number of summers ahead. It is terrible how quickly time flashes by. Let this realisation motivate you to act, let the preciousness of your remaining time give you a sense of urgency. Your fear will disappear to be replaced by an overwhelming desire to make the most of your life.

My mortality makes me aware that I must be very selective about how I use my time and my energy. Mortality teaches you to put things into perspective. There is no need for drama. Simply distance yourself from petty, daily stress. Once you make the decision to act, it will be easy to ignore irrelevant needs and pointless obligations. My sport did a good job of teaching me that. I recognise all too well that you can put things out of your mind any time and any place.

When my son was born, I wondered if it was worth continuing to take big risks and I asked myself why I was doing it and if it was still necessary? Was I still in search of recognition? Did I keep on doing it for myself or for the media and for my sponsors? Was it possible to combine it with my new role as a father?

I thought about it for months, I still think about it. I came to two conclusions. First, even if I were to quit, there is no guarantee that I will live to be ninety-five. I could have a heart attack or be run over by a car tomorrow. The line between life and death is very thin, much thinner than most people believe. Second, who do I want to be for my son? What values do I want to give him? What I do is who I am. I want my son to remember his father as passionate, as a man who gave his all for what he believed in and for what he wanted out of life.

'Stand for who you are!'

I am not interested in my son following in my footsteps, doing exactly what I do. I am more concerned about his core values and that he follows his dreams. I want him to do what he wants to do with his life, to be passionate about what he does and to be fulfilled by his life.

A few years back, I needed my reserve parachute for the very first time in my life. I had made over 10,000 jumps by then over the course of the preceding twenty-five years. I never imagined that I would have to use my reserve parachute one day.

That was a so-called clutch moment, that split second when everything, and in this case my life, was suddenly at stake and the only chance you have is to keep cool and make the right decision.

At such a moment, it is not exactly helpful to be paralysed by fear.

We were flying out of a small airport in Belgium, testing a new wingsuit. The weather was beautiful, there was no wind. All conditions were good. I jumped out of the plane at 12,000 feet. In my sport it is very important to have a safety margin and even after 10,000 jumps I was still not so complacent that I threw all caution to the wind. Even now, I still make sure I have enough time to respond if something goes wrong.

Then something went wrong.

My main parachute opened weirdly, very abruptly and jolted me very powerfully.

Baff!

I did not lose consciousness, but it took me a couple seconds to re-orient myself. The lines of the parachute were pushed against my throat so that I could not move properly. I saw something was wrong but did not know what it was. That was the worst thing: I had no idea what had gone wrong.

Had I not packed my parachute correctly? Although I was plummeting towards the earth, fortunately I was still high enough to have about one minute to gather my thoughts and think it through. I was very calm and rational. I did not feel fear and I did not panic, there was simply no time or room for that. And moments like this one are those when you can rely on your experience and skills.

I knew what had to be done and I knew I had a reserve parachute. I had never used it, but I thought, "Let's see if the reserve works."

First, I had to release my main parachute. So, I came back into free fall for two seconds. Then I opened the reserve parachute.

It opened but very slowly.

I always wear a helmet with a video camera, so I was able to look at a film of the jump later and could see that it seemed to take forever for that reserve parachute to open. But I had quickly solved my problem. Otherwise you would not have this book in your hands.

Although I remained very calm during the whole procedure, all kinds of negative scenarios jumped into my head afterwards. What if I have another parachute failure, what if I totally lose my orientation, etc.?

What still bothers me now is that, to this day, I do not really know what went wrong, why the main parachute failed. That was a mindfuck for a long time.

Had I made a mistake? Was that a sign that I should have stopped? Was it evidence that I had become complacent? What if something like that happened again? These questions created some sort of blockage. I had to pause everything. I told myself, "Wow, hold on! Cedric, you are totally distracted."

It is not that I became complacent. Not at all. But I was forced to ask myself the question: did I still want to deal with that stress?

To check that mindfuck, I asked myself what was the worst thing that could have happened. "Okay, your parachute wouldn't open, but was that the end? You had a reserve for that very circumstance."

Eventually, I regained my confidence and my positive mindset. I rely very much on numbers and statistics. That is a way to rationalise my fear. A classic example is that many people are afraid of flying, but according to the statistics flying is still the safest way to travel. Driving is much more deadly. I can think very rationally. I have solved every problem that has arisen in the past thirty years. This way of thinking let me put my clutch moment on the shelf.

Every now and then, that mindfuck still pops up in my head. All I need to do is to visualise how I solved that problem. The more control you have over your fears, the better you can control yourself when something goes wrong. That helps you to believe that you can control any situation. Therefore, no matter how destabilising your clutch moment was, experiencing one and surviving it is educational.

So, there you are. You have an answer to the question, "How do I control myself in difficult moments and how can you let go of fear?"

Before an emergency even happens, it is good practice to imagine the worst-case scenario for every step of a process. For example, you want to do something, but you are afraid that you will fail. What is the worst thing that could possibly happen to you when you take the first step? Often this exercise demonstrates that there really is nothing so terrible that could happen.

What about the second step of your process? Is something bad possible or not? Repeat this evaluation for each step of the process. If something does not work, you can always take a step back. Well, not always, but often.

This sort of thinking should be part of your overall preparation when you take risks. Take it from someone who has made risk taking into his life: good preparation and repetition is a lifeline. The better I am prepared, the more calmly I can react when something goes wrong. This gives me a much greater sense of control over a situation.

Anxiety and fear are unpleasant emotions, but at the same time they have a clear function. When we are afraid, it is usually because our brain says, "I'm not ready for this!" The stress of a difficult exam is a negative voice that says, "You're not ready!" Good preparation silences that voice.

'Preparation proceeds mastery.'

It is crucial that you are capable of accurately estimating whether you are well prepared or not. When I feel that my preparation is not 100 percent, I step back. That is not always easy. External pressures can push me to step forwards. Sponsors, media, peer pressure and, not to be underestimated, my ego, are powerful forces that push me to jump and take the wrong decisions.

Sometimes it is more difficult to say no than it is to jump. If I have strong feelings of doubt, I force myself to review the situation and then come back later, much better prepared. When I say this to people, they sometimes ask, "At what point do you typically realise that you are not ready? How do you know?"

Good questions. I have only one response: when I feel doubtful, I analyse my doubt using two main criteria. The first criterion is, how intense my doubt is, and secondly, I ask myself what my intuition tells me. The results help me to decide if it is the right time to jump or not.

I do not have a magic formula for making my decision, it is something very personal. That is my *fingerspitzengefühl*, meaning it is my ability to read a situation, an ability derived from experience and self-awareness that has evolved into intuition. Someone with strong intuition can sense a situation better than others, but only experience teaches you whether your intuition can be trusted.

When there is a big decision to make, it is common to run through alternatives in your mind, both consciously and subconsciously. These internal debates have a huge impact on what we eventually do. Unfortunately, our brain usually listens most closely to the doubtful voices, as in: "What if I fail?", or "What if I lose my job?" or "What if people don't like me?" and so forth.

Stop!

When something goes wrong or when we have to perform under pressure, it is very easy to send a negative message to yourself. You must counteract this by building a positive inner dialogue. Many top athletes do this. A positive inner dialogue and visualisation are two techniques you can use to dispel your fear. When your fear disappears, your self-confidence increases.

1. Visualisation or mental imagery

Many top athletes visualise a victory. Our brain does not make a difference between imagination and reality, so visualisation is a very a powerful tool for programming your brain for success. Football players prepare for matches by visualising the perfect pass. Golfers see themselves performing their swing perfectly in their minds and then follow the trajectory of the ball as it flies through the air, lands on the green and drops into the hole. Formula 1 driver Ayrton Senna was incredibly good at visualising and knew just how he would tackle each curve on a race-track before he slipped behind the wheel.

Brazilian football legend Pelé was renowned for his imagination and planning. He developed a ritual to prepare for a match. Pelé isolated himself one hour before the start of each match. He would hold a piece of cloth over his eyes so he would not be distracted and played a three-part film in his mind's eye.

First, he pictured himself as a child, playing football on the beach with his friends. He used this image to rekindle his connection to the sport, his love and passion for it, the why of football. He created a good feeling in his mind. In the second step, he visualised all his victories to remind him of his capabilities and create a strong and positive mindset. In the third and final step of his preparation ritual, he envisioned himself playing on top form in the coming match and pictured his team winning. These three steps brought him into the mindset of a victory.

I prepare in a similar way.

Before any jump, I visualise my line of flight, the flight line I want to follow. I try to imagine it as a perfect trajectory, like a racing driver does when they enter a straightaway. I imagine my parachute opens nicely and how I will land. I visualise the satisfaction that follows, so that I see myself with a big smile. This is a means to boost my self-confidence.

'Yes, I did it!'

This technique is frequently used in sports psychology but can be applied in all areas of life. If you visualise yourself in a very successful situation and imagine yourself being confident and well prepared you will take a lot of weight off your shoulders.

I have never felt I needed an end goal, but I have always imagined myself in very positive situations and I do that to this day. I imagine myself as a partner, a speaker, an athlete and perhaps also a writer within three years. In my mind's eye I have been walking around with a book, my book, for years. It will happen, I know it!

2. A positive self-dialogue

'Your words are powerful.
Be careful how you talk to yourself.'

Everything you say to yourself has a huge impact on your actions. Our lives are defined by our thoughts, so if you are very aware of what you are thinking, you are also going to do much more consciously. The more you become aware of this, the more control you have over your words and ultimately over your actions. It is quite simply a mind game.

I am ready to jump. I know it's dangerous, but I must fill my brain with positive thoughts. I can say, "I'm going to die, this could be my last jump," or, "I'm well prepared, I'm looking forward to it, I'm going to do this because I believe in myself."

You should always defer to the voice that says, "I can do it, I'm looking forward to it!" This way you create a positive mindset. This is how most top athletes and top entrepreneurs generate a particularly strong mentality.

When I accompanied the Belgian national football team, the Red Devils, I asked: "How do you deal with fear? Do you feel fear before you start a match?" One of their star players, Axel Witsel, replied, "I turn fear into excitement." Thanks to a positive inner dialogue, Witsel makes a choice in the fight-or-flight response: "Let's do it!"

The best antidote to fear is action. You must dare to take the first step to suppress your fear. If you can train yourself to confront your fear and step outside your comfort zone, you will discover a level of freedom that most people will never experience. You will grow as a person. Suddenly you will see many more opportunities and possibilities.

'Freedom lies in being bold.'

Overcoming your fear is the highest form of freedom, even more than physical or financial freedom. You follow your own path. You dare and so you push back your limits. That is the first step to making your dream life come true and achieving your goals.

'Your dreams are on the other side of fear.'

If you want to be free, you must embrace uncertainty.

For me, base jumping symbolises ultimate freedom. At the same time, it takes a lot of discipline, or that freedom will mean death. That may sound paradoxical, but freedom *is* paradoxical.

Freedom can be dangerous. You must impose rules on yourself, otherwise you cannot use that freedom. The more freedom you have, the more discipline you need to control it and to stay in control. If you do not manage your freedom, freedom will control you and you will no longer be free. But do not let that put you off. It would be too ironic if by achieving freedom you became afraid to be free.

You do not have to jump off a building to confront your fears. For someone who is an introvert, like me, speaking to a stranger is an incredible risk. Trying something new is always a risk. The idea is to make the unthinkable the new standard and that unthinkable is different for everyone<.

A STATE OF FLOW

Have you read *The Rise of Superman* by Steven Kotler? It is not about an alien with superhuman powers, but about extreme athletes like me. Kotler asks why extreme sports have evolved so much compared to mainstream sports. I do not fully agree with his position, because cycling, football and tennis, for example, have also evolved enormously. But I do agree with Kotler that the evolution in extreme sports is the result of flow. Susan A. Jackson and Mihaly Csikszent-mihalyi have also written an excellent book about the benefits of flow entitled *Flow in Sports*. What impact has flow had on human athletic performance?

Let us look at the bigger picture: Humans have roamed the earth for over 150,000 years. Yet in the last thirty years, men and women from a wide range of disciplines have pushed the boundaries of human performance further and faster than ever before. How did we make such headway in this relatively short period of time? It may be due to flow.

What is flow? Flow is the state in which you deliver your best performance with optimal awareness.

'A state of peak performance and optimal consciousness.'

Athletes who practise adventure sports keep pushing the boundaries. For them, flow is the key to survival.

'It's a question of survival, it's flow or die!'

In a state of flow, you are fully absorbed by what you do, and at the same time, you let go of everything. You are not concerned at all about what you are doing. Physiologically, when you get into the flow, your conscious mind bypasses the prefrontal cortex, that part of the brain devoted to identity, self-criticism and self-control. So, when you are in the flow, you are aware of what you are doing, you can assess it and correct it, but you do not overthink it. Flow lets you avoid paralysis by analysis.

Csikszentmihalyi's writing on flow captures my experience of flying. Flow is the perfect balance between anxiety and boredom, meaning that you are free of nervous energy but not to the point where you become bored. Flow is the point where optimal performance meets optimal consciousness. You seem to be in a tunnel where everything happens much more slowly than otherwise, and time becomes distorted

During moments of flow you become so involved in the action that you no longer think about how to do it and whether you will succeed or fail.

> 'There's this focus that, once it becomes intense,
> leads to a sense of ecstasy, a sense of clarity:
> you know exactly what you want to do from
> one moment to the next; you get immediate feedback.'

— Mihaly Csikszentmihalyi —

Flow has played a critical role in many of the most impressive performances. One of my passions is to explore how a radical mental attitude enables people to redefine the limits of what is possible. My goal is to crack the code of ultimate achievement and I want to do that by bridging the gap between the extreme and the mainstream.

That's why I call myself a flow hacker.

More than anyone, adventure athletes have propelled flow hacking forwards. If we can decipher precisely what people do when they are in flow, we can apply that knowledge to everyone. We could translate their insights from the extreme to the everyday context.

A state of flow increases creativity, drives innovation, accelerates learning processes, improves memory and improves happiness. If you could create an environment of flow in your life, your job or whatever you do, you will automatically perform much better. When you get into that flow, you become much more aware of what you do, you enjoy it more and you get a lot more satisfaction and fulfilment from it.

You don't have to jump from buildings or fly in a wingsuit to experience flow. Top athletes also experience flow and you can even experience flow in your job or in everyday life, wherever it may be.

Flow is about not allowing fear in the now.

> 'If you are depressed, you are living in the past.
> If you are anxious, you are living in the future.
> If you are at peace, you are living in the present.'

— Lao Tzu —

Most people can, at times, be anxious about what the future holds. The anticipation of an event or situation about which we know little can make us fearful. When this happens, we stop thinking about the present.

If you are engaged wholly in the present, you eliminate the anxiety and fear about the future and increase your ability to optimise your performance and to be happy. Or in other words, the more you are in the moment, the less anxiety you have and the more you will be connected to your environment and what you feel – and not so much with what you think.

Before I jump, I do feel fear, because I know what can happen. But that fear disappears as soon as I fully surrender to the action, to the now.

Top athletes deliver their best performance when they are completely in the now and can let go of everything. That is the foundation of flow.

'Being in the present.'

The first step to flow is getting into the now. One of the tools for this is meditation. Make no mistake: everyone meditates, in their own way. We all have ways to bring peace to our minds, you do not have to go to a monastery in Tibet for that. We must demystify meditation.

Ten years ago, everyone laughed when I spoke about meditation: That is for hippies! Times have changed. At Google HQ, there are now meditation spaces. Every employee is asked to stop what they are doing a few times a day so they can calm their brain. By stepping out of the operational, you become focused, productive and sharp again.

'Slowing down to go faster.'

We are all on a carousel. You can see something nice across the street, but you cannot reach it, because the carousel keeps turning. Sometimes you need to stop the carousel and walk across the street. This way you calm your brain and you work much more efficiently.

When your computer crashes or freezes, what do you do? Reset it. Our brain sometimes needs that too.

Find the moment to hit reset. Find it now.

Meditation embraces a very wide spectrum of approaches, there are many different variants. It always comes down to asking yourself: what brings me back to the now? What is calming my brain? It could be walking or running that puts you in a meditative state.

Meditation can help you be in the now. The more you are in the now, the more resilient, the more creative, the calmer, clearer you can think, the more balanced you are and the better you perform.

As described above, flow is a powerful state of consciousness. To understand, analyse and apply a state of flow, it is important to see what happens in the brain when you are in flow or about to go in flow.

During a state of flow, five performance enhancing substances are released in the brain: dopamine, norepinephrine, endorphins, anandamide and serotonin. They are substances that convey information across neurological and other biological pathways. They play a role in our physical performance and our mood and can give us physical and mental strength. Let us look at them one by one.

Dopamine

Dopamine is the neurotransmitter that makes us feel happy. It is strongly related to rewards. Dopamine is released when we surrender to something that gives us pleasure.

Dopamine creates the very human tendency to constantly search for new experiences and environments. Do you feel great when you experience something new or when you get somewhere you've never been? Then dopamine engulfs your brain.

It increases your heart rate and blood pressure and makes your muscles contract faster. Dopamine increases our attention and our ability to process information and recognise patterns.

Thanks to dopamine, we can concentrate better on what we do and at the same time it makes us feel very good about it.

Norepinephrine

Norepinephrine plays a similar role to dopamine in the experience of flow. It boosts our heart rate, muscle tension and breathing, which greatly helps to improve our performance. Norepinephrine also releases glucose into our bloodstream, so we have more energy.

In our brain, norepinephrine increases the efficiency of the neural network. Our excitement and attention increase, as does our emotional control. From a flow perspective, norepinephrine ensures that we remain focused on our goal and exclude distraction.

People in a state of flow often report experiencing heightened awareness, seeing, feeling and smelling more. With less conscious effort, they process more impulses from their environment. That is due to the cooperation of norepinephrine and dopamine. Those two ensure that you can concentrate better, while feeling great in your body. You will experience a reward for your increased focus and concentration.

Endorphins

The body makes its own painkillers with endorphins. Endorphins reduce the physical effects of stress and decrease the degree to which you experience pain or discomfort. When endorphins are released, your body relaxes, and you feel intense pleasure. The most common variant of endorphins is a hundred times more powerful than the pain reliever morphine.

In a state of flow, that means that pain, tension and stress disappear and are replaced by pleasure. The fact that a state of flow is effortless is largely because endorphins change the way your body responds to pain. As a result, athletes can sometimes continue to perform despite a serious injury – sometimes they don't even notice they are injured.

Anandamide

My favourite ingredient of the flow cocktail is anandamide. This neurotransmitter's name is derived from the Sanskrit word ananda, meaning bliss. Anandamide binds to the cannabinoid receptors in our brain – yes, the psychoactive compound in cannabis, THC, mimics the action of anandamide. Both substances have similar effects.

Anandamide increases our well-being, soothes pain, dilates blood vessels and airways, and improves our lateral thinking – that is our ability to connect separate ideas so that we become more creative. More importantly, anandamide suppresses anxiety, making it easier to take risks or try things we would not otherwise dare.

Again, we are dealing with a substance that makes us feel good while we experience less pain. Anandamide activates parts of our body that help deliver athletic performance.

Serotonin

Last in the list is our friend serotonin. Although it is not directly involved in the experience of flow, there seems to be some evidence that it is emerging in the final stage of a state of flow. Serotonin gives us the feeling of peace and tranquillity when we have experienced flow.

That neurotransmitter is important because it helps determine our mood. Low serotonin levels are linked to depression, and several antidepressants affect the way our brain processes serotonin.

What a cocktail we have here! Flow is the only time when our brain produces those five signalling substances at the same time.

Norepinephrine sharpens our focus so that we record more data. Dopamine strengthens our ability to recognise patterns and thus process data. Anandamide accelerates lateral thinking, allowing us to recognise patterns in an even larger amount of data. Endorphins help to reduce stress so that we remain calm throughout the process. Also, these effects make us feel great.

> 'A flow state is like taking cocaine, speed, heroine, marijuana, and anti-depressants all at the same time.'

A state of flow is a very powerful mix of the best neurotransmitters the brain has to offer to promote performance. Flow ensures that we perform at our highest level and enjoy it to the fullest.

You cannot initiate neurochemical processes on command, but you can elicit a state of flow. What should we do to release those signalling substances in our brain? We know that new experiences are causing a surge of dopamine. We know that exercise releases anandamide and endorphins. We know that excitement and risk stimulate norepinephrine. All those stimuli form puzzle pieces for the state of flow. Take the right incentives together and you are on your way to flow.

Playing with neurotransmitters, however, involves risks. During flow, the strongest signalling substances flood your brain at the same time, making flow perhaps the most addictive state we can experience. That is also why so many extreme athletes push their limits too far and die. In their hunt to get into a state of flow, the stakes are getting higher. Just because they keep raising the bar to achieve flow, it becomes increasingly difficult and therefore more dangerous to get there.

When you exaggerate, you hijack your brain's reward centre. You destroy the system that drives your motivation. That way you disrupt your creativity and your mental skills.

'Play with fire recklessly and you might get burned.'

Be careful when you explore flow. Avoid flow taking control. Pay attention to the addictive side of it and make sure that your urge for flow does not put you in situations that are too dangerous.

'Always flow safely.'

But before you can even taste flow at all, you must first learn how to generate flow in concrete terms. After all, in practice it is not so obvious to get into a state of flow. Fortunately, there are three power skills that help you to find flow and achieve top performance.

ROUND-UP

» Self-awareness makes the difference between good and great.
» Free yourself from your addiction to automatisms in five steps:
   1 Water down your opinions
   2 Take yourself less seriously
   3 Discover your wrong patterns
   4 Recognise the problems you create yourself
   5 Be realistic
» Three levels of self-awareness keep negative emotions away:
   1 What distracts you?
   2 Why do you do what you do?
   3 Where are your blind spots?
» Hard work speaks for itself: without an effort you will get nowhere.
» Watch out for the Performance Paradox and the Growth Paradox, which are the dark side of performance. Perform only because it gives you satisfaction, not because you must perform.
» Confront your fear and convert negative fear into positive fear.
» Overcome your fear in three steps:
   1 Accept fear and stress
   2 Give up control
   3 Trust yourself
» Become aware of your mortality to neutralise fear of failure.
» With every step you take, consider the worst consequence: usually that is not so bad.
» Use these four methods to boost your confidence:
   1 Visualisation
   2 A positive self-dialogue
   3 Preparation
   4 Intuition
» Embracing uncertainty brings freedom. In this way you make the unthinkable the new standard.
» Be absorbed by what you do and immerse yourself completely in the now: this way you experience a state of flow.
» Flow is a state of optimal awareness in which you deliver your best performance, with maximum satisfaction.
» Free your head and step out of the daily grinder to reset your brain.

Powerful questions

» What are my biggest fears today?
» What is holding me back from achieving my goals today?

2

FROM A FIXED TO A ROCKET MINDSET

'You must be willing to let go of who you think you are to discover whom you can become.'

TOWARDS A MINDSET WITHOUT LIMITS

'The only limits you have, are the ones you set yourself.'

For me, it all starts with the right mindset.

Your mindset makes the difference between success and failure. It is as simple as that.

"What attracts you most as an investor?", I asked an English businessman at a London start-up event. I was curious about his selection criteria. "Are you looking for the best idea or the most stimulating concept? Or are you looking for the most competent people with the best training and most advanced degrees?"

He shook his head and said, "I am looking for people with the best mindset. That makes all the difference and that's the only thing that I'm looking for." It is good to have talent. Talent is partly inherited, and it is influenced by our environments. But talent alone is not enough. You must also have the right outlook on life. I always say::

'Your mindset shapes your attitude.'

When my son jumps off the couch at home, people sometimes say, "Wow, he is not afraid of anything, just like his father." On the one hand this is funny, but on the other hand I think it is terrible because we tend to judge behaviours. I was quite cautious and thought things through. I was not particularly talented nor mentally strong. In fact, people may have thought that I never would be. Not me.

I was not born a risk taker; I became one because I wanted to. I saw risk-taking as an opportunity to grow as a human being. I have always looked for ways to make myself better and learn new skills. I have always strived to turn my weaknesses into strengths.

This is what I call a rocket mindset.

Psychologists tend to categorise people as having either a fixed mindset or a growth mindset. People with a fixed mindset do not believe that they are able to grow or do not see a need for it.

Many top athletes and entrepreneurs who are extremely talented and skilful never live up to their potential because they lack the right mindset. By contrast, many relatively less talented but determined and hardworking people rise to the top of their field because they have the right mindset.

This distinction is clearly seen amongst young footballers. Kids with tons of talent are often not the ones who break through, rather it is the ones that work the hardest that end up with wonderful careers. Someone who plays for Inter Milan, Barcelona or Real Madrid is not necessarily more talented or skilful than someone playing in the Belgian first division. Their distinguishing characteristic is a dedication to maintain constant high levels of effort and their openness to personal growth.

Those at the pinnacle of the sporting world, like Tiger Woods or Roger Federer and their counterparts in the business or artistic world, clearly possess the necessary skills to rise to the top, but the quality of their mindsets is the characteristic that they share. They have the complete package it takes to be successful and achieve their dreams.

My son is a quick learner and I am not always happy about this. He reads at the level of kids two years older than he is, and the school gives him extra support for that. However, if he is confronted with a task that requires any real effort, he sometimes becomes blocked and complains, "I can't do this," whereas another child might say, "I'm going to find a way around this in the long run." This worries me. We need to teach our kids that the quality of our effort is more important than the result.

School results matter, but what matters most to me is that children understand that dedication and hard work will help them overcome any obstacle.

'For children with a rocket mindset,
the sky is the limit when it comes to life's possibilities.'

Children with a rocket mindset do not necessarily want to be the first, they get satisfaction from pushing their boundaries and increasing their potential. They are aware that they must train and work hard to achieve top results, dedication is almost a matter of course.

The good news is that you can, literally, change your mindset, even though the term "fixed mindset" sounds so restrictive. The way we are "wired", neurologically, has a strong influence on our character, but we can influence this. We can change the physical route that information takes as it travels through our mind. This means that we can teach ourselves to modify our response to a stimulus. This ability to change the way our brains process information is termed neuroplasticity. There are few things that we can control in life, but we have full control over our mindset, and it is our mindset that shapes our faith in our ability to achieve. It colours our perception of ourselves and of the world around us.

'Our mindset shapes our belief
in accomplishing something.'

This is what I want to teach you.

'Become limitless with a rocket mindset!'

'You are not defined by who you think you are.
The possibilities to change yourself are endless.'

'Life is about change and growth, nothing is permanent.
Everything is subject to change.'

'Being is always becoming.'

People with fixed mindsets are convinced that their talent and skills are predetermined, that they are fixed and can or will never change. They think, "I was born this way and I will die this way," or, "my father was like this and I accept that I am the same."

I have friends who want to start their own business but discard the idea out of hand, saying "I am not from an entrepreneurial family, my parents are teachers and civil servants, so I just don't have it in me." They are self-limiting.

All of us have self-limiting thought patterns. We must be aware of them if we want to overcome them. If not, we risk being unwitting victims of our environments.

Our mindset is strongly influenced by our environment. Parents and teachers play a very important role in a child's development. Children who grow up surrounded by people with strong limiting beliefs, adopt this mindset.

My teachers told me several times that I was not a good writer and I came to believe this. A child who hears fifty times that he is not good at sports will eventually believe it. Yet, we are born with rocket mindsets. Very young children are receptive to learning, they constantly try new things. They squeeze toys and bite everything. Unfortunately, this natural response diminishes over time.

Consider a seven-year-old who says that they want to become an astronaut and is told, "No, that is not possible." When I was seven, I announced that I wanted to fly. My teacher tried to convince me that my dream was impossible. Had I accepted her opinion, I might not be doing what I am doing now.

Self-limiting thought patterns are also an issue in work environments. We hear a lot about transforming corporate cultures, but transformation can only occur if limiting patterns of thought are identified and altered.

Make no mistake: we all have limiting beliefs. Even the most accomplished among us suffer from it. Our limiting beliefs make us hesitant to act. They lead us to making comments such as, "I don't have the right skills," or, "the timing's not right." Even if both comments are true, what is stopping you from learning new skills and adjusting the timing?

You can only become better as a person or as a manager if you learn to counter your restrictive thinking patterns. You may be thinking, "All well and good, but a rocket mindset just isn't 'me'".

Nonsense.

Everyone can acquire a rocket mindset and make the previously unthinkable the new normal.

Champions are not born. They are made.

How can you develop a rocket mindset?

This is how:

» Be open to constructive feedback
» Train your brain and commit to a lifetime of learning
» Challenge and push yourself

I used to think that I was not a good speaker, that I should not crawl onstage to talk about my ideas. Fifteen years ago, a friend asked me to give a talk at his company. I could have thought to myself, "No way, I can't do that, I don't have the talent or the skills for that." Instead, I remember thinking, "Speaking in public isn't exactly one of my strengths, so how can I learn to become a good public speaker."

The only way to learn how good or bad I was at public speaking, was to just do it.

'Life doesn't get better by chance, it gets better by change.'

— Jim Rohn —

I used this mindset to break through a restrictive thinking pattern that had haunted me since my school days. I would toss and turn all night if I had to speak in front of the class the next day.

Breaking through my limiting beliefs enabled me to transform the unthinkable into my new norm.

Self-limiting beliefs simplify our lives. They protect us from touching hot stoves. But if we establish too many limiting thought patterns, our lives become dull. Imagine if after a painful break-up you allowed yourself to believe that love only brings doom and grief. You might protect yourself, but you would also prevent yourself from experiencing something beautiful.

A particularly insidious thing about self-limiting beliefs is that they filter our reality without us being aware of it. As a result, everyone's reality is different, simply because our self-limiting beliefs differ. This explains, for example, why one person can laugh in a situation that other people find very disturbing.

Many people believe that their view of the world reflects reality, unaware that their self-limiting beliefs dictate that the world they see is only true for them. Our biased perspectives are very difficult to recognise and to overcome.

How can you discover your own limiting beliefs?

When you hear yourself say things like "I'm the sort of person who...," or "I can't do this," you can be pretty sure that you have found a self-limiting belief that does not necessarily reflect reality. Is there an activity you do not enjoy? This says more about your thinking pattern than it does about the intrinsic value of that activity.

Some self-limiting beliefs are very difficult to discover because they were incorporated into your view of the world early in your development. They may have been transferred to you by your parents. Even if these views no longer serve a purpose for you, they will continue to colour your experiences and perceptions. You may not be aware of them and so they remain intact in your psyche.

However, self-limiting beliefs do not have to last forever. You can get rid of them by keeping a close eye on your stream of thoughts. Whenever a negative thought pops up, ask yourself about the source of your response and why you would think so negatively about something. It can take a long time to expose your self-limiting beliefs, but it will be time well spent. Your quality of life depends on it.

Be aware: you are no longer a child and you have free will. You can choose to stick to restrictive thinking patterns or to change them. It is up to you.

If you choose to cast off a self-limiting belief, it will be easier to do if you have evidence to refute the belief. You will need to try to believe in that rebuttal and you must have faith that your life will be enriched by your action.

For example, if you think that you will never make a lot of money, you must force yourself to believe that you can make yourself rich. From that point on, look at every cent that you earn as proof of your abilities.

Remember that a self-limiting belief can seem to be justified because people tend to unconsciously register experiences that support the belief.

For example, if someone believes that they are unlucky, they tend to dismiss or not even recognise evidence to the contrary. So, you must keep your mind open to facts that invalidate your self-limiting beliefs.

You are completely free to choose which life to live. Only you can decide what you believe in and how you behave. Apart from the influence of mental trauma, you are solely responsible for the person you have become. If you shift that responsibility to other people, you lose the power to change your own life. That is not a wise decision.

Being fully accountable and taking full ownership of your actions is the first and most important step towards transformation. You then have the opportunity to put aside your self-limiting beliefs and develop a rocket mindset.

'Complacency is the fastest way to obsolescence.'

For people with a rocket mindset, the sky is the limit. Such people are convinced that they can achieve anything they want if they remain open to questioning themselves, to learning new skills and to growing. This is easily seen in children. When a child with a rocket mindset is presented with a difficult maths problem, they do not run away from it, they take up the challenge. Such children are eager to be challenged more and progress faster than other children.

People with a rocket mindset are convinced that they can still evolve and change. They view failure as a learning process. Imagine that you made an error while filling out a spreadsheet. People with a fixed mindset say to themselves, "I'm so sloppy." People with a rocket mindset say to themselves, "How can I avoid making the same mistake again?"

A rocket mindset allows you to see challenges as opportunities for growth, as a chance to learn from the best. This is something I do too. I always try to surround myself with people who are more capable or skilled than I am.

That goes against the instinct of people with a fixed mindset. They unconsciously surround themselves with people who are less skilled or capable than they are. We do not like to fail because we do not want to be judged, it is bad for the ego. This makes them feel superior and it protects their ego. But do they grow? No.

Three common traits in people with a fixed mindset are:
1   They are not open to feedback, especially if it is negative. They seek confirmation of their ideas and compliments.
2   They become quickly frustrated and give up when faced with failure.
3   They avoid challenges and ask, "why should I change anything?" It's the epitome of complacency.

In my world, complacency is deadly. Complacency leads to a loss of focus. When you avoid challenges you lose your edge, you stop growing and learning. I have seen a lot of people crash because of complacency. Those people fell victim to their ego.

Many people start new undertakings with enthusiasm, but once they reach a certain level in their endeavour their appetite for learning and personal development can diminish. They may reach a certain level of name recognition and the prestige that goes with it and then become overconfident in their abilities. They come to believe that they are invincible.

And then they make a mistake that they pay for with death.

A strong and healthy ego is not necessarily bad, but there is a very fine line between self-confidence and the dark side of an over-inflated ego.

A friend of mine used to be an F-16 pilot and instructor with the Belgian Air Force. Every time he took on a new student, he warned them:

'If you wanna stay alive in this environment,
stay below your skills.'

That rule has saved me many times.

I always operate just below my competences. This gives me a margin, a learning zone, within which I stay. I have thought of myself as a student from an early age and I always will. There is always something new to be learned, even from people who have been in the sport for far many fewer years that I have. The fact that I have jumped so many times does not mean that I know everything.

One thing that I know for certain and beyond any doubt at all is that when you are driven by your ego, it can be fatal. Never cross the line between self-confidence and ego because this is a very thin line.

It is all too common to find complacency, enormous egos and fixed mindsets within companies and organisations. People fall easily into the mistake of saying to themselves: I've been doing something my way for twenty years, it works, so I will continue doing it for another twenty years.

A few years ago, I gave a workshop on risk management to surgeons from a hospital in Belgium. Afterwards, one of those surgeons came to me for a chat. "One of our biggest problems is complacency," he said. "Many surgical blunders result from this. Over-confidence can lead to bad habits in a surgeon and this can lead to errors that are often fatal."

In the business environment and especially in times of disruption, complacency is the fastest way to obsolescence. Complacency can lead to a person becoming ineffective or even dangerous. Companies that do not keep complacency in check are setting themselves on the road to failure. The average lifespan of companies listed in Standard & Poor's 500 was sixty-one years in 1958. Today, it is less than eighteen years. It is predicted that by 2027, 75% of the companies currently quoted on the S&P 500 will no longer exist (McKinsey).

BlackBerry, Nokia and Kodak were once market leaders in their segments. They were the standard against which all their competitors were compared. Yet they disappeared from the market at lightning speed. Business analysts and former senior managers at these companies concur that a culture of complacency lay at the heart of their demise. Complacency allowed them to fall behind technological developments and to lose touch with the demands of consumers.

The consequence of complacency is always the same: you become irrelevant, then obsolete and then you no longer exist.

People with a rocket mindset continuously seek out opportunities to learn and they continuously train to maintain their skills. They recognise that it is not enough to be good at something to stay good at something. They do not allow complacency a chance to compromise their lives. They are passionate and committed. They remain motivated.

Not all of us has a passion. For many people, their work and their passion are different and not even complementary. Even the best performers in the world are not always motivated.

In fact, the point is not to find your passion. The point is to first find your purpose, your "Why".

So, how is it that some people remain passionate, committed and motivated in the long run?

The key is knowing why we do what we do. A clear understanding of why we are driven about something gives our lives a purpose, a meaning, and it motivates us to carry on pursuing what we do over the long term.

PURPOSE: THE POWER OF WHY

'The great secret of passion
is an emotionally compelling purpose.'

People with a rocket mindset are purpose driven. Such people have a very clear idea of why they do what they do and what they want to achieve. I cannot stress enough how important this is. Knowing why you are doing something makes it much easier to grow from a fixed to a rocket mindset.

That is the Power of Why.

'If you find your "why", then your "how"
and "what" become clear.'

Organisations, top athletes, entrepreneurs and even students need to be motivated to succeed. If they lose touch with the essence of what drives them, they lose the urge to exert themselves and the quality of their performance declines.

Full engagement is necessary, but how do you sustain your motivation?

Let us talk about passion. I am very passionate, but I think that word is used too often. After all, most of us do not have a job that is also our passion.

But, if you have a very clear purpose, you can create passion.

Steve Jobs, co-founder of Apple who revolutionised the computer industry, was not necessarily passionate about technology. He had a very strong purpose: to bring a computer to every household. This purpose drove the phenomenal growth and success of Apple.

Elon Musk, founder of Tesla, PayPal and several other breakthrough companies, is not at all passionate about cars or finance, but he has a very clear purpose and that is to progress the evolution of the human species in a positive direction via innovations in business. He is quoted as saying that each of his ventures was a means to that end and that the enormous wealth that he amassed along the way was a side-effect of following his passion, that wealth was not his goal. Tesla is more than simply a producer of electric cars; it is also a company that breaks the mould in its business concept and practices.

When I started giving lectures, I was not passionate about speaking to audiences and it terrified me. But I did it, nevertheless. Why? To push myself and because I was curious. I accepted the uncertainty it involved and put aside my ego.

With time, I became passionate about giving lectures. How did this happen? Because my purpose was very strong and very clear: to inspire people to become the best version of themselves, to act and make their dreams come true.

That is my passion. That is what enables me to continue to speak to an audience with great enthusiasm. When I speak, I am on a mission. I want to make an impact.

Why Power is the basis of my commitment. It is what motivates me.

My Why Power has two components:

1   To push my limits and see how far I can go as a person.
2   To show other people that if I can push my limits, they can too.

Defining your purpose may seem selfish at first, because you are doing something for yourself alone. There is nothing wrong with this. You must be able to breathe before you can give oxygen to others.

After passengers are boarded and seated on a commercial flight, the flight attendants demonstrate what to do in case of an emergency. You are told that oxygen masks will drop down from the ceiling and that adults should put on their masks first and then help children with their masks. It seems counterintuitive at first, but it makes sense. You need oxygen to help others.

When I visit companies to give presentations, someone in the audience invariably remarks that what I do is selfish, that it jeopardises the security of my family. I tell them very directly that I do not agree and that I made and continue to make a conscious choice about what I do. My son is far better off having a father who is frequently at home, who is totally committed to what he does, and who is happier than he would be if he came home late, sullen and frustrated because he was not following his dreams. By oxygenating myself, I oxygenate my family.

Having a purpose in life not only motivates you, it is the foundation of a rocket mindset. With a purpose-driven mindset, you can go much further and grow as a person much more easily than other people.

Companies that have a purpose that is understood by, meaningful to and embraced by staff and management alike, have a powerful advantage in the market. Is Ikea's purpose selling furniture? No. Ingvar Kamprad's objective when he founded Ikea was to simplify people's lives and this ethos remains intact at Ikea today.

The company Red Bull has a clear motivating purpose: giving wings to people and ideas. This purpose is understood by everyone working for Red Bull, worldwide. Red Bull is the epitome of a purpose-driven mindset culture.

How do companies go about engaging all their employees in the company culture? The starting point must be to define the company's mission, its

purpose. In other words, it must be clear why the company exists at all. From a broader perspective, what will be the legacy of the company, what will be your legacy?

'What's my legacy?'

I put the following question to Philippe Rogge, President of Microsoft Central and Eastern Europe: "If you were to leave your company, how would you want to be remembered?"

His reply was compelling: "As someone who helped the people around him to grow. I want to create leaders from the people around me."

That is leadership. It is also a good example of a strong purpose for senior managers and CEOs.

Leadership is not a tool to ascend a hierarchy, to attain status and a title. Having a title does not transform someone into a leader. Leadership is about knowing how you can make a difference to individuals and to the environment in which you all operate. That is the essence of leadership. This perspective on leadership means that everyone can be a leader within an organisation, a team or even a family. You can establish and develop your leadership skills by asking yourself: how can I inspire others; how can I instil positive values in those around me and how can I help them and these values to flourish?

The success of other people can be inspirational. When I mentor people like the renowned chef, Sergio Herman, I feel a true sense of excitement and think, "Wow, I'm going to push my own limits even more!"

When I asked Sergio what his purpose was, he replied without hesitation, "I want to offer people a unique experience and make them happy."

If you have a very clear purpose you will be more easily inspired, and you will be more inspiring to others. Also, do not be discouraged by your limiting beliefs: you know how to manage them.

Base jump (with permit) from a windmill in Hungary.

POSITIVE RITUALS

In order to rid yourself of self-limiting thinking patterns you must identify what is causing them. Frequently, it is down to our daily habits.

'People are creators of habits.'

The actions that we repeat daily become our habits. These habits give a certain direction to our lives, they shape who you become and your destiny.

'We are what we repeatedly do.'

The lazy reaction to this predicament is to stick to your old habits, outmoded as they may be. This means that you accept your limiting beliefs. You will never grow as a person with this attitude.

Habits provide a safety zone, but a safety zone is a kind of cage from which it can be difficult to escape.

Awareness of the power of the unconscious to guide and change our thinking and our behaviour is the first step towards transforming our habits and ultimately to transforming our lives.

Shifting from a fixed mindset to a rocket mindset, in contrast, requires a lot of self-awareness. It entails stepping out of your comfort zone, something most people do not like to do. You must become aware of your old habits, break them and replace them with new positive ones. This can be an energy draining and very painful process, but the more ground you travel towards a rocket mindset, the more fascinating and the less painful the transformation becomes.

Step One – Identify and demolish negative habits
We can use the Triple A technique and become the observer.
» Awareness: recognise your negative thinking pattern
» Acceptance: it is okay to feel bad!
» Action: react and create positive thoughts

Step Two – Define and establish positive habits
Remember, in psychology we say that negative emotions stick like Velcro in the brain and positive emotions glide like Teflon. For highly resilient and mentally tough people, it is just the opposite. Negative emotions glide like Teflon!

In the lexicon of applied sports psychology, positive habits are described as performance routines. Every top athlete has a very clear routine before an important competition.

Earlier in this book, I described Pelé's performance routine, how he isolated himself for one hour before each match to visualise his childhood, his previous victories and the upcoming match. This enabled him to begin every match with a very strong, positive mindset.

I also have a performance routine to prepare for each jump. I isolate myself and check all my equipment, in a fixed order. Then I check the weather conditions and then I ask myself how I feel, if I feel good. Even closing my zippers and hearing the sound are part of my routine and enable me to be fully focused.

I never deviate from this procedure. Positive habits are my way to ensure my safety, just as a pilot runs through a safety checklist before taking off.

Most successful people also have a morning routine, which is often a very powerful positive habit. The way you start your day has a huge impact on the rest of that day. Many studies show, unsurprisingly if you think about it, that people who check their social media and emails immediately upon waking are less productive than people who do not. Social media and emails mainly create anxiety.

Successful people make a conscious choice about how to initiate their day in a positive, balanced way and they usually get up earlier than others. This is not always easy. Few people are willing to get up at five in the morning every day without a good reason. But, if you want to go where few people go, you must do things that few people do. By starting your day very early you get a head start. You are much more productive in the early hours because you will have much less distraction.

Our brains are primed to be most creative during the first hour after we awake. The prefrontal cortex, that part of the brain that controls planning, decision making, social behaviour and other complex functions takes about one hour to become fully awake, so we don't overthink things in that time-frame; we can avoid paralysis by analysis. We can let our thoughts flow with less stress than later in the day. During this first hour, neurotransmitters such as dopamine and serotonin begin to course through our brains, (see the last chapter for a refresher). A morning routine is a way to achieve a state of flow, the optimal state of peak performance. A morning routine is a route to creating a flow mindset. Eventually, you will enter this flow mindset out of habit.

'Flow is the elite mindset to all top performance.'

Finding the morning routine that suits you best is a matter of experimentation. I favour this test and learn approach. I adjust all kinds of things all the time to find out what works best for me and what does not.

For example, sleep requirements vary widely between people. In my view it is wrong to say that everyone needs eight hours of sleep. For some people, four hours may be enough, while others need nine hours of sleep to feel rested. We need to listen to our own bodies to decide how much sleep we need.

I took a cold shower for years. This did not appear to help my immune system, but at least I tested this.

I follow what is known as a bulletproof diet, where you avoid saturated fat in favour of polyunsaturated fat and reduce your sugar intake. I admit to melting a knob of butter in my morning coffee. At the time of writing this book, I am waiting to see what effect this diet will have on me.

My morning routine can last two hours and sometimes only lasts half an hour. I usually wake up on my own between six and six thirty – I don't set my alarm unless I have an early morning appointment. Every morning I meditate for half an hour to create space in my head.

An example of my morning routine:

» **6.00:** Wake up, without an alarm clock, and meditate.
» **6.30:** Make coffee – with a knob of butter. I am a big fan of bulletproof coffee and intermittent fasting.
» **6.40:** Review my gratitude list. This is a moment of reflection, to consider my gratitude for my life and the people around me, to appreciate my health, freedom and the simple fact that I live and breathe.
» **6.50:** Define my priorities for the day. When I am at home, I write it down. When I am on the road, I do this exercise in my head. I ask myself very consciously: what is the best use of my time and energy today?
» **7.00:** Look at my mobile phone for the first time and start exercising.
» **8.00:** Take my son to school.

Your morning routine may look completely different. The point is that you need to find a way to start your day that best suits you. You may even just read the newspaper and drink coffee. If that works for you, great! Stick with it.

A morning routine that is not good for anyone is: to be startled awake by your alarm, to push snooze, to be woken again by the alarm, to push snooze again and so forth until you finally drag yourself out of bed and then frantically rush about to make it to work on time.

It is important to start your day in a very calm, intentional way and to ask yourself each morning, "What are my priorities today? How can I make a difference today?"

A good morning routine is a source of peace that also prepares you for an exceptionally productive day.

One of the advantages of getting up early is that you can use the solitude to make the most of your mental state prior to the pre-frontal cortex coming into action. A period of planned solitude helps you to centre yourself, it is your holy hour.

We all have a certain mental capacity, a cognitive bandwidth, so to speak. We are subjected to stimulation and sometimes over-stimulation throughout the day. Relevant and irrelevant information is flung our way, we work, we process messages and we speak to colleagues. It never ends. All that distraction demands attention and eats away at our mental space. Our mental bandwidth narrows.

In the first hour of the morning, however, we have our full mental capacity. By getting up early you can give your full attention to something that is very important to you – even something like reading a book. Or you may wish to meditate, or learn something new, or exercise. The goal of this first hour after waking is to create energy. When this has been accomplished, you are ready to pick up your smartphone and read your emails.

Turning your morning routine into a positive habit will make every day much more productive. You will become more focused and efficient.

RESILIENCE AND LETTING GO

'Mental toughness is the ability to face adversity,
failure and negative events without losing your motivation.
It's a relentless determination to achieve your highest goals
in tough or difficult times. It's something you can control.'

Resilience is another element of the rocket mindset. Purpose defines why you get into a rocket; resilience keeps you from becoming stuck on the launch pad if your rocket does not blast off on the first try.

People with a rocket mindset are exceptionally resilient.

Resilience is an amazing skill to have, especially in times of crisis. We build our resilience by learning to cope with challenges. It is a process of adapting well in the face of trauma, failure and stress. Over time, successful people learn not only to overcome but to embrace these challenges. They understand that each crisis they face is an opportunity to grow, transform and learn.

There are two aspects of resilience that serve a rocket mindset. Resilience prevents you from getting hung up on things and it helps you to let them go. Resilience also keeps you from being discouraged after a setback or even after numerous setbacks.

1. Letting Go

Imagine you are frustrated. How quickly can you let go of that feeling?

Most people have many expectations and often unrealistic expectations. They expect everything will go their way. But because life is inherently unpredictable, things do not always go as expected and so their unrealistic expectations inevitably lead them to bouts of frustration.

People with a rocket mindset can deal with setbacks quite differently because they are resilient. So, they do not become disillusioned or frustrated. Their resilience allows them to maintain a general sense of happiness at work and in their private lives.

When I mentor football players, I always ask how they feel when something goes wrong in the first fifteen minutes of the match. Most admit that they find it difficult to put such set-backs out of their mind and say that their mindset becomes negative.

It is only those who are at the top of the sport, for example the Argentinian footballer Lionel Messi, who can immediately let go of their frustrations and start over with a clean sheet straight away.

It is extremely important to let frustration, anger or sadness pass quickly. It is not wholly accurate to classify these emotions as only negative, because they do have a function. They can alert us to a problem or danger. But they can cause a problem if such emotions occupy too much of our thoughts. When that happens, when we become distracted by emotions, they can put us in danger instead of protecting us.

So how does one deal with these negative emotions? Feel them, accept them, learn from them if needed, discard them.

2. Bouncing Back

Resilience is also about recovering after failure, bouncing back. Okay, you failed. You learned from it and you move on!

This is the way resilient people operate. Resilience enables top athletes to return to the top much faster after a setback, such as a serious injury.

I can let go and be back in action very quickly after a setback. I am very conscious of this and I recognise that this is partly due to my nature.

I accept that this may not be such a straightforward process for many people who have never learned to let go and bounce back. An inability to bounce back can lead to mental fatigue, bitterness and serious psychological and physical consequences.

ACCEPT UNCERTAINTY AND PUT IT TO WORK FOR YOU

The moment you look for certainty, you give up on your dreams!

When people with a fixed mindset fail, they immediately give up.

If someone with a rocket mindset fails, they see it as part of a learning process. They keep trying, not because they are stubborn but because they are perseverant.

People with limiting thought patterns exist in their environments and ask no questions. They filter the information that comes their way to gain confirmation of their point of view. Such people see themselves as a finished product, not as the current version of a continuous process.

'People with a fixed mindset assume, they don't ask.'

Those who are stuck in a fixed mindset look for excuses, complain about things over which they have no control and never take responsibility for their actions. Such people prefer to avoid difficulties.

People with a rocket mindset are eager to develop. They know they can only take steps forward when they question what they already know. That is why they consciously look for difficulties and challenges, because they know that this is the only way to grow.

People with a fixed mindset usually envy the success of others. With a rocket mindset, you ask yourself, "What do I have to do to achieve the same success? Because I want to be there too." They do not envy others, others inspire them.

When someone inspires me, I do not think they are special or luckier than me. Instead, I wonder: "How did he do it and how can I do the same thing?" I may not get to the same level, but I want to try.

I am convinced that everyone can do anything if they put the right energy and focus into it.

I am not saying that you will be able to excel at everything you try. My point is that you will be able to do it at a level that gives you satisfaction. I am too old to become the new Usain Bolt. But that does not mean I should not try sprinting. My achievement can still reach a level at which I can be happy.

Some things are genetically determined and so they are a matter of luck. For example, tennis players with a strong backhand naturally have good co-ordination between their left eye and right hand. David Goffin is an example. However, he also has weaknesses. Instead of thinking he cannot do anything about his weaknesses, he works to overcome them. His physical coach, Fabien Bertrand, who is a long-time friend told me this a few years ago.

When I started to take more and more risks, I didn't think, "I'm not mentally strong enough for this". Instead I asked myself, "How can I become mentally strong enough to make a success of this and ultimately survive in this high-risk environment?"

If we want to develop a growth mindset, we must allow ourselves to be vulnerable. That also means that we must dare to speak about what we are not doing well and that we become aware of our blind spots. We must drop our mask because that is the only way we can grow.

This is not easy.

A fixed mindset is an emotional crutch. It supports us and protects us from failure. A fixed mindset ensures recognition and brings comfort. Nevertheless, a crutch remains a bothersome thing. We must throw that crutch out and, yes, that is annoying at first.

Someone with a rocket mindset does not cling to his crutch, but asks, "How can I improve? What is the first step?" They accept uncertainty and use it to reinvent themselves and stay relevant in a world that is changing very quickly. If you ask me: "What is the best decision you have ever made in your life?", it was to accept uncertainty! Uncertainty makes us feel alive, common certainty makes you feel asleep. But it was also about embracing and using uncertainty to stay laser-focused, sharp and humble in this type of environment.

'Our mindset shapes whether we believe we can learn, change and grow – or not.'

ROUND-UP

» Having talent is good, but only with the right mindset can you make the most of that talent by realising that you also must work hard.

» Changing your mindset is possible: you can grow from a fixed mindset to a rocket mindset.

» People with a fixed mindset have limiting beliefs. Those restrictive thinking patterns inhibit growth, but you can break them.

» People with a fixed mindset consider themselves a finished product. Combined with a large ego, this leads to complacency.

» Complacency can lead to mistakes, sometimes even death. People with a rocket mindset counter that pattern by always remaining open to feedback and new insights.

» A rocket mindset is a purpose-driven mindset: people with such a mindset know very well why they do something and what they want to achieve.

» A clear purpose gives you Why Power. That is the starting point of all passion, motivation and commitment.

» Limiting beliefs and a lack of awareness often lead to negative habits. With a rocket mindset you can destroy those bad habits and replace them with positive habits.

» All top performers have performance routines, because you do not excel once, but again and again.

» One of the most powerful positive habits is the morning routine. During the first hour of the day you are more creative and more easily reach a state of flow.

» Getting up early and doing something meaningful gives you mental energy for the rest of the day.

» A rocket mindset makes you resilient. After a setback, you let go of your frustration faster and you bounce back more easily to a positive mindset.

» With a rocket mindset, it is easier to take on challenges. If you fail, you consider it a learning process.

» A rocket mindset is about accepting uncertainty.

Powerful questions

» What are my limiting beliefs today? Identify them.

» What is the first step I can take today to reset those thinking patterns?

3

FOCUS IS THE NEW IQ

'Don't waste energy. Focus on what you control.
Not on what you wish you controlled.'

OPTIMAL CONCENTRATION

What do you think when you hear the word "focus"?

I always ask that question when I hold a workshop on focus and most people automatically think about concentration. However, concentration is only one type of focus. Concentration is the ability to focus on a task, to think clearly and perform a cognitive task undistracted. Concentration is *inner focus*.

Focus is about efficiency and productivity, but also about satisfaction and happiness. You may not associate those last two concepts immediately, but I will explain this.

Nowadays, it is very hard to concentrate. Our attention span is getting shorter and shorter – a lot of published research supports this. East Asian youngsters, for example, have difficulty concentrating on one task for more than fifteen or twenty seconds. Modern life is full of ever more distractions, such as smartphones, over which we exert little control. Distractions have begun to control our lives. We don't choose them, they choose us!

Base jump (with permit) of the Atenor Tower in the centre of Brussels. With its 114 metres, it is the tallest residential tower in Belgium.

Distraction is detrimental, but sometimes distraction can be helpful. You cannot be focused twenty-four hours a day, seven days a week. That is simply impossible. Concentration and distraction are reciprocal. Focus is your mental energy. It is not linear; it is a cycle.

There is no need to be constantly focused on your task. Sometimes letting your mind wander and become distracted is needed to be creative. Finding your own rhythm – for example, fifty minutes of concentration and ten minutes of break – is a good way to stay focused for a long time.

Someone who stays focused on their task for a long time becomes much more productive and can do a lot more work in a shorter time. In this way, they have more time for themselves and for the distraction they *choose*. Or they have time to focus on other new projects.

This also means that people who lack focus need a lot of time to finish something and therefore do not have time left for themselves or for other projects.

Sometimes your circumstances do not lend themselves to staying focused for a long time. This is true of many working environments. This is a challenge, because work must be done in the workplace. Yet, often, many people sit together in one room so there are constant distractions.

In companies, the average attention span was three minutes ten years ago, but today, it is only forty-five seconds. That is very little.

Most people today work in *multitasking mode*. People seem to be convinced that they need to do a lot at once. This may be true, but how much of what you do is done right?

It is well documented that multitasking is the enemy of productivity. Some studies have even shown that multitasking damages the brain. British researchers took MRI scans of people who regularly multitask very intensely – for example, watching television and texting at the same time. The brain region responsible for empathy and emotional control was found to have a lower density than normal.

First, multitasking means wasting our time and energy. When we constantly jump from one task to another, we lose focus. If, after completing several interim tasks, we return to our original task, a lot of time will be wasted by re-establishing our concentration.

The result? We stay busy all the time, but never with deep concentration and focus.

In my sport, where concentration is a matter of survival, multitasking is deadly. I must be fully focused on what I do and be fully absorbed in it, or I will die.

For students, employees and creatives, focus on one task at a time or your productivity will eventually die.

How do you achieve more concentration and therefore higher productivity? To do that, you must do two things that are actually very simple.

First, learn to recognise *when* you are not focused. Become aware of the moments when your concentration fails. That is a matter of self-awareness or *Meta-awareness*.

Second, be aware of *what* distracts you. That can be social media, the internet, your phone or a colleague who demands your attention every five minutes. The issue is that you become aware of it, so that you can then channel or even eliminate that distraction.

Elite athletes, artists and musicians are completely absorbed by what they do. The more you focus on what you do, the better. The more flow you achieve, the more productive and efficient you become.

Like everyone else, I get distracted very quickly in a busy environment. I am aware of that, so I avoid busy environments when I want to work.

You focus better on your work when you are alone.

Painter Pablo Picasso said:

'Without great solitude, no serious work is possible.'

When you are alone, you give yourself more room to really think about what is important. In an environment with social bustle, this is not possible.

Brilliant physicists like Albert Einstein and Isaac Newton were very often alone. They shut themselves off from the outside world to think about the possibilities of working out their theories.

Boredom is good for us. Nowadays, the idea is rather that a child who is bored should be entertained immediately. This is not necessary. Letting a child find their own way to keep themselves occupied stimulates their creativity and awareness.

If your schedule is constantly full, you simply do not have time to think.

I use a tool to maintain my concentration: *tracking*. When I am distracted, I write it down, and I write down what distracted me and for how long.

There are many computer apps for time management, but it is best to take notes on your own initiative when you become distracted. You will become aware of when you are and are not focused.

People who can focus on one thing at a time are the people who are making progress.

PRIORITIES: ARE YOU BUSY OR ARE YOU PRODUCTIVE?

When you ask someone how it is going, you often get the answer: "I am busy!"

Many people then ask, "Oh, doing what?"

But the real question being asked is more interesting: "Are you busy or are you productive?"

It is possible to be very busy, without being productive. People who are never focused and do not concentrate, are just busy. They actually do nothing and being busy is for idiots.

People who are busy cannot make choices. They cannot say no. Such people are not selective in what they do and do not prioritise. They accept everything and do too much, including a lot of unnecessary things. They are trapped in a daily operational routine. That is how they lose control of themselves and their lives.

On the other hand, some people are very productive. Such people have *external focus*. What does this mean? People who are very productive are very focused on their priorities. They ask themselves every day: "What can I do today to add value to my life and my work?"

> 'Busy people are masters of yes,
> highly productive people are magicians of no.'

Leaders like Warren Buffett and Steve Jobs are often asked: "What's the key to your tremendous productivity?", to which they often reply that the key is their ability to rule out spending time on things that do not fit their priorities.

> 'What you prioritise tomorrow, will dictate
> what you will do and where you will be in five years.'

I used to want to read a lot, but you get confused if you read too much. As soon as we read something, our brain no longer distinguishes between essentials and afterthoughts. That is why I am much more selective now and I wonder before I open a book: should I read this book? Do I need this information?

Also watching the news is a waste of time and energy. That sounds harsh, but tell me honestly: how often is the news relevant to you? We forget 99 percent of the news a week after we heard it.

In addition, news is often negative, which gives us a pessimistic view of the world and the future or increases anxiety especially in times of disruption and crisis. When employees are fired, that is news, but it is not news when a company is doing well, and employees feel connected to their business. Because of all that bad news, we either become restless or insensitive to what is happening in the world.

Most of the news has no direct impact on our lives. When news is relevant to you, you usually already know about it or cannot change it. In most cases, the news is just something to chat about with your family or at a café. If you do not watch the news, your life will not be fundamentally different, but you will have more mental space and time.

I myself look very little at the news. The result is that I feel calmer and more optimistic. I am not distracted, and I am more actively involved in and connected to what is happening in *my environment*. Read and watch what makes you happy and what adds value. Ignore everything else.

External focus comes from highly selective behaviour. This is something that is out of fashion. Children these days have packed agendas. They must be everywhere; they must do everything, and they should never get bored. But are they happier? No.

Adults also succumb to irrelevant obligations. They do things because they feel they must, not because they want to. This causes them to lose focus on what adds value to their lives.

In our society, it is very difficult to turn down an invitation. We were not raised to do this. Nevertheless, you must dare to make choices and say no without feeling guilty. People prefer to make up excuses for saying no when they should feel comfortable saying, "I just don't have enough energy right now," or, "I just cannot justify doing that right now." If you want to be highly productive, you have no option but to make choices and sacrifices.

A journalist asked Roger Federer, how he had stayed at the top for so long to which Federer replied, "If I focus on my priorities, I will keep winning."

There are four rules of thumb to help you keep focused on your priorities and avoid being busy without being productive:

1   Do fewer things but do them better.
2   Reject the idea that you must excel at everything. Choose one direction in which you want to excel.
3   Ask yourself what your priorities are, which of the directions you could go will yield added value and which will not.
4   Act. Do what you must do and eliminate distractions.

Just as death – or at least the realisation that we will die one day – is a tool against fear of failure, our mortality also helps us make choices. Thinking of death is positive, because that is how we make ourselves aware that we must act.

However, in some people the effect is negative: when they realise that their time is limited, they try to do as much as possible! They try to have it all: money, power, prestige, everything imaginable. Thinking of death can make you restless when you ask yourself, "Have I done enough in this world?"

My message is that very few things are vital to our emotional well-being and to achieve our goals. Again: do less but do it better.

'Cut things out.'

Think of the sculptor who gets a block of wood or marble. He does not add things, but just chops things away to reach the essence.

When I talk about essentialism, people often think of the material, of having less. But for me, that concept goes much further. It is about doing a limited number of things with more intent.

It is also necessary for companies to concentrate their energy on their priorities. Companies that are not focused on their core activities lose their way very quickly.

In the 1990s Starbucks suddenly started selling a lot of things in addition to their core product, even CDs and TVs, things that have nothing to do with coffee. That is how the chain squandered its core identity. And then the trust of the customers evaporated.

Growing companies often lose their focus because their own complexity and bureaucracy preoccupies them to the extent that they lose sight of what their priority was.

You see the same thing in people climbing the corporate career ladder. They are very driven and focused at the start. The higher they climb up through the hierarchy, the less time they spend working on the thing they once thought was a priority: they lose their focus.

The reason for being selective and doing fewer things better is not only to increase productivity. The reason is that if you are selective you will focus on the things you get satisfaction from. Only then can you be productive.

For businesses and entrepreneurs, the same principle applies – *simplify, simplify, simplify*.

Focusing on your priorities sounds easy, but how do you determine what they are?

Simple:

Make a list of the twenty things you want to do in your life.

Out of those twenty, select five that are priorities.

Then delete the rest, because you will never have the time to do them.

Another technique to make better choices is to ask yourself what the added value is of the activities or projects where your participation is requested. If they offer no added value, then stay away.

Sometimes, however, this added value is not always clear.

What is clear is that you are in doubt about something. When I doubt something, I know it is not a priority. If it is crystal clear that I want to do something, it is a priority and otherwise I will not start.

By focusing on your core values you will remain who you really are.

THE KEY TO ACHIEVING MASSIVE RESULTS

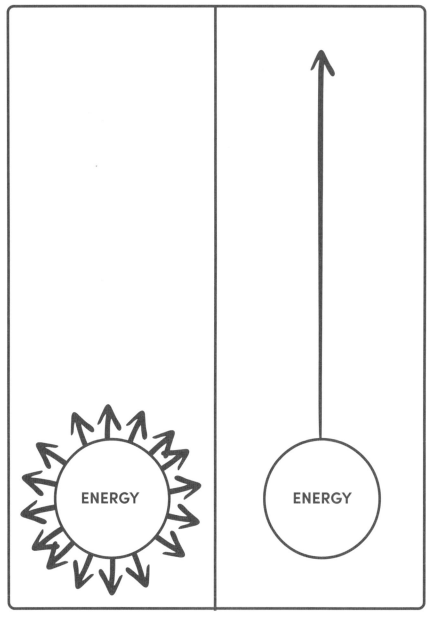

~~PURSUING EVERYTHING~~   FOCUSING ON ONE THING ✔

The way we organise our lives and our work is very old-fashioned. It is based on time.

We live in a society that encourages all of us to fill our agendas. If there is an empty space in their agenda, many people think: Hey, I am not maximising the use of my time.

Even if we do not feel like doing something or if we do not have mental energy for an activity, we feel obliged to participate anyway because we are afraid of being judged: what will people say if I do not have a full agenda?

You need to get rid of that pattern of thought.

If you want to focus more on what is important, you need to create air and space in your calendar. This can only be done by dropping the things that are not important.

My focus on priorities has always been a very strong point. Every day, every week, every month I ask myself, "What are my top priorities now? What am I doing today, this month and this year?"

I have been using this approach for so long that it has become a habit. It is part of my way of thinking. It is one of the most important ways to stay true to who I am. Asking myself these questions prevents me from losing myself in things that are not efficient or relevant.

Sometimes – very rarely – a week looks a little empty. Then I still feel a tendency to accept a few meetings or calls.

Doing!

This is when I must remind myself that filling my agenda with low priority meetings will not make me more productive. It will not add value to me.

Top entrepreneurs and top athletes are constantly receiving requests from all kinds of people who want something from them. And for a lot of people, it is hard to say, "No, I am not interested."

I have never had a problem with that.

'Keep it simple.'

By saying no and focusing on what is important, you make everything easier.

'Don't ask yourself what the world needs!
Ask yourself what makes you come alive.
Because what the world needs
is people who have come alive.'

— Howard Thurman —

A form of focus is knowing what makes you happy as a human being. That could be something in your job or in your personal life, if it energises you.

A lot of people think in time, I think in energy. It is all about energy, everything comes back to that. It is incredibly important to focus on that.

We all only have twenty-four hours a day. You cannot create more time, but you can create or leverage your energy to make it seem like you can, and the more energy you have, the better use you can make of your time.

Why do we procrastinate? Because we lack energy. This can be physical, emotional, mental or spiritual energy. Spiritual energy is about your purpose, about the *Why Power*. If you do not know why you should do something, you simply have less energy for it.

That is why you must ask yourself every day: what gives me energy?

'What fuels me?'

When I talk about this, some people say, "Okay, but you can't *always do* what makes you happy?"

That is true. Sometimes you must make a sacrifice and do something that does not immediately make you happy. But there is no contradiction in that, it is about the difference between pleasure and happiness.

Pleasure is a matter of instant gratification. It is a neurochemical reaction involving the release of dopamine into the brain. You feel it when you buy a car or when the parcel service delivers a new pair of shoes. Fun is fun, but it does not make you happy. Sometimes a few hours later you can already regret things that you enjoyed at the time.

Focusing on things that make you happy goes much deeper than looking for fun. Your happiness can arise from success, making progress in acquiring certain skills, or helping people. Sometimes – even often – unpleasant things need to be done on the path to happiness. It is not always easy. Not everything should be *enjoyable immediately*, but it takes perseverance to keep moving forward when things get a little tricky.

Top athletes spend all their time and energy getting to the top of their sport. They may make huge sacrifices along the way, but it leads somewhere: to satisfaction and fulfilment. Without satisfaction, there is no point in working hard.

People who have adopted a rocket mindset have fewer problems persevering than people with a fixed mindset. They do not give up; they know that fulfilment awaits them once they overcome the difficulties.

If we try to do too much in our lives, we make ourselves unhappy.

Unfortunately, we live in a society where there are a lot of opportunities. The choice is so great that choosing becomes difficult, which makes us want to do too much. That is how we become stressed.

We are under a lot of pressure to want everything. We want to be a good partner and parent, we want to be ambitious and have a great career, we want time for ourselves and we want a busy social life at the same time. The result is that we lose ourselves in all these things, because doing them well and all at once is impossible. Why are there so many divorces? Partly because people are not focused on their priorities.

Fear of Missing Out (FOMO) is a big problem for many people. I see that even with some friends of mine: they want to be involved with everything, but they are not happy and certainly not fulfilled.

Base jump with a wingsuit from the Jin Mao Tower in Shanghai (421 metres). We had been licensed by the Chinese government but were only allowed to jump at night. One of my most intense experiences.

What I see very often in companies is that people invest so much time in their work that they lose sight of their families. That leads to unhappy children and a disgruntled partner. Those people are losing sight of what is important in life.

It is better to learn what makes you truly deeply happy. What are your priorities?

The reasoning behind this is very simple: you cannot get good at something if it is not your priority.

Top athletes only do their top sport. They may miss out on doing a lot of other things, but they get satisfaction from their successful careers.

I have had to make hard choices, too, for example when I said to my friends as a teenager, "I'm not going out, because I have to train tomorrow." At the time, that may not have been nice, but in time that choice never made me unhappy. I knew exactly where my focus was!

People should go more for JOMO, the Joy of Missing Out. Sometimes you have to say, "This is not important, it has no added value. I don't care about it."

It is important to be focused on a goal. If you want to achieve a goal and if you do things with intent, you keep your focus.

But!

You must make a distinction between the end goal and the process of getting there. Having an end goal is fine, but at some point, you must be able to set that aside to focus entirely on the process, on the road that leads to your goal.

People who focus only on their end goal and not on the process put themselves under enormous pressure. Focusing only on the end goal or finish line can make it seem too far off and unattainable. This way of thinking leads to the belief that you will never reach your goal, so you do not take pleasure in the activity, you become frustrated and ultimately you lose control of the process as you create anxiety for the future.

This is a common problem: people live with their mind on the future, worrying about deadlines or the results they need to get. This problem is compounded because they are constantly given new objectives and targets.

People say things like, "If I can reach my financial target, I'll be ok," or, "After I buy my dream home, I can relax, and I will be happy." These people become addicted to their end goals and can no longer enjoy what they do and the process of getting there.

That is the dark side of achievement.

It is OK to have a vision, perspective and projects but we do not live in the future; our lives are happening now.

'Life happens in the present moment.'

You must enjoy what you do while you do it. How else can you get satisfaction from your work?

Therefore, set aside your end goal and focus on micro-goals. This approach will lead you eventually to your end goal and the whole process will be much more manageable.

Daily goals have a huge impact. By making the right choices every day, you influence the result. This results in a *compound or cumulative effect*, where every small step in the right direction reinforces the effect of the next step.

Imagine that you are writing a book – a process I have become familiar with lately. I could have said to myself, "I will write twenty pages every day!" But that is a lot. I do not have the mental energy to write twenty pages every day. So, instead I could have said, "I'll try to write more tomorrow." And the next day I could have said to myself, "Damn, I just do not have enough time for that."

What if I had decided to write *five* pages every day? That is not so much, but if I were to write five pages, two days in a row, I would have a lot more text than if I had put the work off until I could write twenty pages in one go.

Once you find a sustainable rhythm that you can stick to, you should be able to write an entire book in the long run. Suddenly you should find a thick stack of paper on your desk, without you worrying, "How on earth am I ever going to write a whole book?" You will enjoy the process much more.

In the workplace, many people create unnecessary stress by worrying about the future of their business, constantly asking themselves, "What's going to happen, and will I still have a job next year?"

When you think this way, you are not doing yourself any favours. My recommendation is to focus and dedicate yourself to the here and now, because you have no influence or little control over what will happen in the future. If something does go wrong, you will know that you have done everything possible to keep your job because you remained focused on the process and you did not lose energy through worrying.

A few years ago, a friend of mine who does free diving wanted to break a record. He was already world champion, but he wanted to dive even deeper. I called him a few weeks before his attempt and asked, "Do you think about your record and final depth before you dive?"

"No, thinking about that would paralyse me," he said. "It would suffocate me."

"What do you think about then?"

"I think of every heartbeat, every breath, every metre. The more I focus on the process and the road to the record, the more likely I am to break the record."

He achieved his goal and broke the record.

Mountaineers also tell me they never think about the summit along the way. They focus on every step they must take or every metre they must climb. If all goes well and if the weather is good, they will reach the summit.

If I have a new project involving risks and I think about the final goal, I will block myself and think, "Oh, that's way too dangerous." But if I divide such ideas into micro-goals, I will get there, step by step. When something goes wrong, I stay much more agile. Then I take a step back and choose a different route and way of progress. Working with micro-goals is therefore also a matter of remaining flexible and agile in an often volatile and uncertain environment.

The more you work in an incremental process, the more flow you create. You become so focused and absorbed in the action itself that you stop being concerned about the result. You are not just busy; you are also productive.

We have come across this principle before: detachment from the outcome. You hardly care about the result because the process itself gets your full attention.

Instead of stressing about the future and the end goal, I am totally focused on the now. The more dedication I live in the now, the more I can trust the future.

Sometimes I think, "In five years, it will all be over. I will not be asked to speak anymore; I will not sell any more books, and no one will want to be mentored by me anymore."

But if I give 200% of myself each day, I know everything will be fine five years from now.

FOCUS ON WHAT YOU CAN CONTROL

In my environment, I am constantly confronted with volatility and uncertainty. How I deal with this is a matter of choice. I can focus on the problems or I can focus on possible solutions.

This is a subtle difference, but it is fundamental. You can choose to focus on things that you cannot change, or you can focus on things that you yourself can improve, on what you can control.

Athletes and businesspeople who focus on things they cannot change become victims of their environment.

You can see that in people who are always negative. They complain about external factors, such as traffic and weather. But by doing this they do not change their situation and only make themselves unhappy. They might as well prepare themselves better or explore how they can avoid these unpleasant conditions.

Within organisations, people often complain about external factors, like the company culture, the management, or some colleagues, you name it. But what do they achieve by complaining? Sometimes we find ourselves in situations over which we have no control. But the way we look at such situations and respond to them is always under our control.

The conclusion is: we always have a choice. It's what we call cognitive reframing:

'It's not about what's happening, but how you frame it.'

You can always view an event or situation in a different way. And only then can you change something.

Complaining every day about traffic or your company's culture will not prevent you being stuck in traffic jams or improve your working environment. In fact, complaining can even magnify your discomfort. If your mindset is fixed you will fail to acknowledge and change the role of your behaviour in creating or amplifying the problem. Fortunately, we already know that our mindset is one of the few things we can always control, so we can change that.

A statement often attributed to Mahatma Gandhi sums it up nicely:

'Be the change you want to see in the world.'

The first person you can change, and control, is yourself.

Within a team of top athletes, you sometimes hear players complain about one another. That is not what the real top players do. They focus on themselves and how they can change themselves. Such people have much more impact on their team than those who complain.

A few years ago, I was leading an expedition in Peru. The project was to base jump from the Gocta Cataracts, a waterfall in the Amazon forest that ranks as one of the highest in the world. We went there with a team of about fifty people. We had a lot of equipment with us and three doctors. There was no room for a helicopter to land, so evacuation by air was not possible. We travelled there by land and on rivers so hospitals would be difficult to reach. It was not an ideal place to break a leg. After ten days, travel in trucks, then by boat and finally by a long stretch on foot we arrived at the site where we decided to set up our base camp. It was quite humid, and the roads were muddy.

The Gocta waterfall in Peru, the second highest one in the world (after Salto del Angel in Venezuela), is difficult to reach, and has an altitude of 850 metres. That we could make two jumps from this waterfall was also a world first. The waterfall is a magical and mythical place and remains one of my most beautiful experiences.

But we got there.

And then the rains started belting down. In a few hours, everything was submerged. We were stuck. We were cut off from the outside world. Even the satellite phone did not work.

Jumping off the waterfall was impossible, because the flow of the river was far too rapid, the current was far too strong, the turbulence was much too intense.

I was the expedition leader. My message to everyone else was, "This situation is beyond our control. What we can control is how we view the situation and how we get back home – alive!"

At first it was not easy to be stranded there. Our food and drinking water supply were limited. We didn't know how long we would be stuck.

Despite these tough conditions, it was my job to bring and maintain everyone in a positive mindset.

Eventually the rain subsided and after two weeks at base camp we were able to start making our way back. It was impossible for me to base jump, but that was the only thing that went wrong. No one had been injured and no one had died.

If you want to, you can let everything annoy you. You can become agitated by colleagues who talk too loudly when you are working or a myriad of other things. Imagine the huge potential there was for annoyance amongst fifty weary and soggy adventurers stranded in the Amazon jungle. Yet our group got on well. In fact, eight months later we made a second attempt and the team consisted of the same people.

This was possible thanks to the third *power skill*:

Trust.

ROUND-UP

» Concentration is inner focus: it is your predisposition to perform a cognitive task without being distracted.

» Distraction is often detrimental, but sometimes your brain needs distraction to catch your breath. If you choose *for yourself*, you can be distracted. Do not let distractions choose you!

» Multitasking is deadly, by reducing productivity, and for adventure athletes, also quite literally deadly in the physical sense.

» Staying focused is done by sequestering yourself. If anything distracts you, write it down, make yourself aware of it.

» Focus is not simply the ability to concentrate, but also the ability to be selective. In our hectic society, it is important that we focus on the things that make us happy and energise us.

» Pleasure is not the same as happiness. If you are pursuing happiness, you sometimes must do unpleasant things. The reward for that is a sense of satisfaction.

» External focus means focusing your attention on your priorities. You may choose not to do some things, and you will then be more productive doing what you chose to do.

» Be selective and do only the things that add value to you. Everything else is a waste of time and energy.

» The process of achieving a goal is more important than the goal itself. If you stay focused on the process, you will reach your goal.

» Forget the end goal and focus on daily, achievable micro-goals. Making the right series of achievable micro-choices every day helps you move forward much more effectively than stressing about a big and seemingly unattainable end goal.

» Some circumstances are unpleasant. If you cannot avoid the unpleasantness, there is no point getting wound up over it. The best way to manage this is to focus on what you can control.

» One of the few things you can control in all circumstances is your mindset and the way you look at things.

Powerful questions

» How long can I keep focused on a task? What distracts me?
» What is my priority today?
» What are my three main goals and what is the first step I can take to achieve my goals?
» What are the three things – or people – that energise me?

4

CREATING TRUST

'If we trust each other, we win together!'

THE FORMULA FOR TRUST

I was wearing my wingsuit and ready to jump off a high rock. My cameraman was right behind me, also in his wingsuit. Just before I jumped, he whispered in my ear:

> 'If you die, I die.'

Was that bad timing? Certainly!

But he pointed out that he trusted me completely and blindly.

That is literally true: when a cameraman flies behind you, he does not look where he flies, his camera frames you, he sees only you. He follows you, and if you make a mistake and crash, he is going to crash, too.

This is an example of what we call terrain flying: flying very close to the relief, with high risks. It is probably the most extreme form of flying, with very little margin for error. Location: the Hinterugg, also known as "The Crack", in Walenstadt (Switzerland).

Trust is crucial in an environment where there are major risks. Otherwise, you are going to die.

My cameraman's announcement did not upset me. My preparation was good, and the conditions were perfect.

I thought, "Here we go!"

Everything starts with trust.

Whenever you try something or do something, it is about trust.

You are your own product. To sell yourself to others, you need to establish that you can be trusted. Your reputation depends on it and this is crucial in a work environment. Likewise, you need to be able to trust people: those you work with, your friends, everyone with whom you undertake something meaningful.

This reciprocity or network of trust is described by psychologists as systemic psychology. This concept considers how we affect and influence one another as well as the interplay between the numerous networks in which we are all involved. When viewed in this fashion, we realise that even those who physically work alone do not work alone in the psychological sense.

Trust is strongly connected with the quality of the result of your performance, and how you perform. You need to demonstrate your ability to be yourself at work and in your private life and show reliability and credibility to be considered authentic and trustworthy. Others view us as authentic and sincere when our goals, actions and values are completely aligned. Without this, trust is not possible.

Without trust, you do not make the most of the skills and potential of the people within your team.

With trust, you can create a safe environment for growth, learning, testing and for thinking outside the box or even for failing in organisations, without the fear of being judged. If you cannot trust the people around you, you can never be entirely yourself. You will not be able to reveal your vulnerability and it will seem to you and to others that you are wearing a mask.

You need to connect with the people you work with.

People need to trust one another to feel safe about being open and confident enough to give and to take feedback, even when it is constructive feedback.

A very clear example can be seen in Formula One. I once got a chance to observe Red Bull's Formula One race team. They have the best technology, impressive resources and skills and an abundance of highly motivated and competent team members. But what I found most striking was the level of trust between the team members. It was trust that made the difference, it was trust that made them such consistent winners. They trusted each other so implicitly that no one wasted time double-checking other people's work. Everyone knew exactly what to do and did it.

I was not at all surprised when Red Bull broke the world record for the fastest pit stop in the autumn of 2019 during the Brazilian Grand Prix. Max Verstappen's tyre change took just 1.82 seconds. The previous world record was already held by Red Bull – and was less than a year old. How did they achieve this? Simply by a high level of trust.

Researchers have analysed the role of trust in organisations. One study showed that in companies where mutual trust was high, employees experienced on average 74% less stress at work, and had 106% more energy than employees that worked in low trust environments. Productivity was boosted by 50% and absenteeism was reduced by 13%. Employees were 76% more engaged and felt a 29% higher level of satisfaction overall with their lives and burnout was reduced by 40% in trust-based companies. If you have been exploring how to develop a climate of trust in your company, you will have learned about the importance of proximity, credibility and reliability.

Unfortunately, we are taught to mistrust others from an early age. Most children are warned repeatedly, "Don't talk to strangers!" This is a valid warning to keep children safe, but it can lead to disproportional levels of distrust with some people becoming unable to trust anyone.

Putting trust in others involves taking a risk and taking risks requires courage. Sometimes you must take that risk, because that is the only way you build a team.

Trust is also complex.

Ask people if they want to be trusted and everyone will reply: "Yes, of course!"

But ask those same people if they trust everyone and they will answer with equal conviction: "No, of course not."

See? Trust is hard.

Certainly, within organisations and companies, trust is a thorny issue. There is a lot of talk about empowerment these days. People are given autonomy, but can they work autonomously if they lack confidence?

"How can I be happy at work if I can't trust anyone senior to me?" This is a comment I have heard many times. One of the consequences of micromanagement is that everything is monitored. When everything is checked, the message is that the people being checked are not trusted.

So, the crucial question is: how do you build trust within a team and empower your people?

Fortunately, there are tools to strengthen confidence and confidence is needed to take the risk to trust.

'Talk the talk, walk the walk.'

Leaders need to take the time to get to know people. That means that sometimes you must suspend your daily operational activities to get to know your colleagues. "I want to get to know you" is a message that surprises people, but it also delivers a huge boost to a person's confidence.

The Belgian division of a large retail chain recently appointed a new HR manager. She said, "I want to get to know everyone on my team." This paid off. People trust her now, they overcame their mistrust and learned to speak more openly with one another. This, in turn, facilitated their ability to work

On our way to base jump from the Gocta waterfall in Peru, enjoying a unique view of the Amazonian jungle.

autonomously. It is a simple, but often overlooked, approach for encouraging trust and improving teamwork.

A company also needs to get to know its customers. What are their needs? What do they expect? The better people know you, the more your customers will trust you. This builds customer loyalty and a competitive advantage.

Young entrepreneurs certainly need to be able to build a network. To do this, you must be reliable and consistent. You cannot build a strong network without people trusting you. Impossible.

Consistency is what connects your words to your actions. If you promise something, you must deliver it. Managers who promise things but do not keep their promises immediately lose the confidence of their employees. What you do has to match what you say. When you propose a strategy, you need to also explain if and how the strategy might change in response to a change in circumstances. If you are not open about this, you will be judged as inconsistent and others will lose their confidence in you if you need to change your strategy. Within a team, trust is very motivating. If you demonstrate that you trust people, you will bring out their best qualities and improve the quality of everyone's work.

'Surround yourself with those
on the same mission as you.'

Working with people who have the same background as yours is easy. But we live in a time of globalisation. Increasingly, teams are made up of people with diverse backgrounds, different cultures and with different ways of thinking, different ambitions, different ages. This can make working together problematic because sometimes people think and behave very differently.

A common goal brings everyone together.

Two film crews accompanied me on my expedition to the Gocta Cataracts: an Argentinian crew to film a TV show and a German crew from Red Bull. Each production company had a completely different way of working. In the beginning there was little empathy between the teams and lots of friction. The Germans were very insistent on efficiency but were less spontaneous than the Argentinians. The Argentinians were very creative and improvisational, but they were not very well organised.

I said at the time, "If we want to work together, we have to accept our differences. Not everyone works the same way and we don't have to stress about it."

Afterwards, they communicated clearly about their way of working and about their expectations, which ultimately led to good cooperation.

At football clubs, coaches must often deal with very different cultural differences. Players from some countries need to be forced to finish their training, whereas other nationalities must be treated very gently, or you will be resented for being too brusque.

Cultural differences are also very interesting within companies. These differences may seem difficult to deal with at first, but a diverse team is a mirror of the society we live in and enriching for an organisation.

I try to work with people who think completely differently from me. That makes my team much richer. But, when I leave on an expedition, I want us all to go in the same direction, for the same purpose.

In 2015 I flew in a wingsuit over the great pyramids in Egypt. During the preparation I worked with Egyptians and that was initially very difficult. My expectations were different from theirs. Their sense of time was also completely different. I am quite punctual – or try to be – but in Egypt they are much less concerned about punctuality. At first, it was hard to deal with. But I thought, okay, I will adjust.

It took empathy on my part to try to put myself in their place. I recognised that we had the same goal and that despite a very different way of working, we shared the same vision and mission. In the end, they proved to be very competent and efficient people, their way of working was culturally different.

Our shared goal was to get a permit to fly above the pyramids and we eventually succeeded. Without them, I would certainly not have been able to pull it off.

A shared goal strengthens mutual trust. Knowing that you are all going in the same direction ensures that you do not have to doubt the motives of the others.

'The moment you accept total responsibility
for everything in your life is the day you claim
the power to change anything in your life.'

In the spring of 2019, I led a team building exercise with the Red Devils, the Belgian national football team. I asked their head coach Roberto Martinez: "You have incredible players, but what's your biggest challenge?"

He replied, "I have a team of stars and in a very short time, I have to make a star team."

"How do you do that?"

"The first thing you've got to have between players, is trust," he said. "If we trust each other, we win together."

This is true of all teams, in companies as in sporting teams.

The Red Devils team has young and slightly older players. Some players have bigger egos than others, they come from different cultural backgrounds, they are at different career stages and different ambitions. But they all influence the performance of the team. If they trust each other, they get off to a good start, despite their differences.

There are two points that Mr Martinez, insists on very strongly: *ownership* and communication.

Ownership means that each player needs to be fully responsible for everything he does.

'You own your actions.'

If something goes wrong, do not blame it on external factors and do not look for excuses. You take responsibility for yourself. It is very important to make players aware of this.

I do, too. If I work on a team, I want everyone to act like a leader. A leader is fully responsible for everything they do and acknowledges their mistakes. That is hard, but it gives you a form of emotional freedom. You are much freer if you can say, "That was wrong of me, I'll admit it."

'Making a mistake is human,
acknowledging a mistake is superhuman.'

I was raised with the idea that I am responsible for what I do. That gives me a lot of strength. Today I find it even easier than I did twenty years ago to say, "Yes, that's my fault."

I used to tend to look for excuses: "Sorry I'm late, there was a lot of traffic." Now I recognise my responsibility and say, "My fault. I left too late."

Taking responsibility is a particularly powerful tool to create trust within a team. Unfortunately, the opposite happens in many companies: "That was not my fault, the company culture is at fault." Or, "It's the manager's fault."

At the end of the day, you always have a choice, you are not just the victim of circumstances. You may not be able to change your business's culture immediately, but you can manage your work in a different way.

For the Red Devils, it was very important that all players became aware of their responsibilities very quickly. Players must acknowledge their mistakes to avoid repeating them in future matches. This is how players win the trust of their teammates.

The idea of ownership is linked to the concept of membership. That means that everyone contributes. It is a tool to strengthen everyone's confidence, because everyone is made to feel valuable to the team. As each member becomes more confident, the team overall gains confidence in one another.

When we were stuck in the Amazon Jungle in Peru, everyone's contribution was needed to think in a solution-oriented way to devise a means of escape while remaining calm and saving energy.

Every individual must ask themselves: how can I make a difference? It may be that you are very technically oriented, but whatever your strength, you can demonstrate leadership through your mental strength.

What matters is that you contribute something.

When someone does not take responsibility and fails to keep their promises, they lose the trust of others.

Can you restore trust if it is violated? Yes, but that is not easy.

When a well-known company loses the trust of its customers, it can fail dramatically. Squandering a reputation sometimes happens in seconds but rebuilding that trust can take years. Volkswagen has still not recovered from the damage caused to its image by the 2015 emissions scandal.

When you are at risk of destroying someone's faith in you, the first step to address this is to take responsibility for what went wrong. It is important that you do not relegate responsibility to external factors, but that you say, "It was my fault." Without this, there is no chance of repair.

After this, there is little else that can help to repair a breach of faith except time.

You can think about what you can do to solve the problem. Can you work harder? Be even more consistent? Any more contributions? You can give even more attention to those points.

Of course, confidence can never be fully restored. That is a pity, but you need to accept reality.

POSITIVE COMMUNICATION

Communication is not just what you say to each other.

Communication has many facets. It is about the words you use to express yourself, the tone of your voice, the timing of when you say something and your body language. Even the way you look is a form of communication.

With the Red Devils, it is very important that they continue to communicate positively and transparently, even if things go wrong. Frustration with one person reflects on the others. This brings negative feelings into your team and reduces efficiency.

Communication is essential to ensure that you know what you expect from each other. In unsettled times, you cannot overcommunicate!

Even if you trust each other, you must continue to communicate very transparently. That is the most efficient way to avoid misunderstandings. Almost all misunderstandings are due to poor communication. If misunderstandings occur too often, it undermines trust.

People say about the company where they work: "We have no idea what the goals are, nor the expectations. Then suddenly we are told that what we are doing isn't any good."

A lack of transparency inevitably leads to misunderstandings. The best basis for any relationship is communication. Sometimes people must dare to speak up for themselves. "Hey, please speak to us, we want to know what is expected of us!"

Communication often goes wrong when too little information is shared. In some companies, every employee and every service try to protect themselves. This tends to make people secretive, to guard information. However, it is wrong not to share information. The more information you share, the better the environment becomes and the more it can evolve. Sharing information can serve a purpose as simple as just confirming that you are not the only one who is struggling. Such insights bind people together.

As humans, we also have a very strong tendency to communicate only when things are going badly. We need to become better at communicating good news, this builds trust. If a manager communicates positively, it is a form of appreciation for everyone. Everyone feels better right away.

If you want to communicate positively and transparently, you may want to consider the benefits of personal communication versus an email. I prefer a real conversation. Why? Because an email lacks the context of body language. Text can be interpreted in many ways, and when it reads badly for some reason, an email has the disadvantage of being reread and badly misunderstood and causing negative sentiments.

Body language is incredibly important, especially in elite sport. Are some players walking around with their shoulders hanging down? Then they make it clear to the whole team that they need to work on developing a winning mindset. It is hard to do when things are not going well, but this is exactly when you must be able to communicate in a very focused and efficient way.

'I believe a good leader brings out
the best in people by listening to them,
trusting in them, believing in them,
respecting them and letting them have a go.'

Wingsuit flight over the Nazca desert in Peru, another world first. I worked for five years to get the permits. A magical location with a strong story and tons of history.

Above all, we need to learn to listen. Listening is the highest form of communication.

Unfortunately, listening has become very difficult. To listen you must be completely in the here and now. When people speak, they immediately start interrupting one another. While one person is still speaking, the other is already thinking about how he will answer.

The result? We do not really listen.

It is difficult to listen to someone *attentively* and intentionally. But if you want to perform as a team, you have no choice but to listen to each other. Also, a leader must be empathetic to really listen.

The better you can listen, the more trust you create.

'Instead of talking about each other, talk to each other.'

— Joe Kaeser, CEO Siemens —

ROUND-UP

» Trust is crucial in an environment with high risks. Without trust, shit happens.

» You must trust yourself, you must trust others, and others must trust you. Without trust, you will not make the most of your own potential and that of the others in your team. Having a reputation for being trustworthy will be your most important skill and asset, enabling you to thrive and survive in a challenging and changing work environment.

» Trust means you can show your vulnerability and be yourself. Trust helps to give each other honest feedback and accept feedback as well.

» Trusting people is a risk, but you need to trust yourself and others to build a team.

» Showing strong leadership skills strengthens confidence. The leader is not the person at the top of the hierarchy: anyone can take up leadership. You do not need a title to be a leader.

» Leaders need to get to know the people they work with and create strong connections with them. Taking the time for that boosts everyone's confidence.

» If you promise something, you must deliver. Otherwise, you will lose the confidence of others right away.

» Teams can be very diverse and consist of people from different backgrounds, cultures and ages. A common goal helps to bring everyone together and strengthen mutual trust.

» Ownership is a powerful tool to build trust. It means you take responsibility for your actions and acknowledge your mistakes.

» Essential to trust is that everyone contributes and thinks about how they can make a difference.

» Trust can be violated very quickly. It often takes a long time to recover it.

» Without communication, there can be no trust. Continuing to communicate positively, even when things are difficult, combats frustration.

» Communication is more than words. Your tone, your timing and your body language play a big part.

» The highest form of communication is listening. Being able to listen attentively and intentionally is the cornerstone of trust.

Powerful questions

» Are my actions in line with my values and goals?
» What can I improve in my way of communicating? Am I a good listener?
» Do I take enough time to get to know people and create connections?
» If I make a mistake, can I easily acknowledge it, or do I blame external factors?

AFTERWORD

Everything you do is a risk.

You do not have to take risks. But if you do not, you will come to regret it because you will have missed a lot of opportunities.

You cannot change anything without risk.

If you do not dare to take risks, there can be no transformation, innovation, creativity and progress.

Do you have to throw yourself into all kinds of adventures? No.

The three power skills – a rocket mindset, a laser focus and trust – make it easier to push your limits.

Developing and growing yourself is intrinsically about taking risks. Remain open to challenges, dare to say no, trust someone: these are all risks.

All our dreams are on the other side of our fear.

Those who are willing to take risks can more easily cope with change, be more innovative and more creative. Failure becomes part of their success.

Someone who does not take any chances will never achieve anything. A company that does not dare to take risks will not even exist in a few years. Be bold or be dead, especially in times of crisis.

There is a strong link between risk and reward. Someone who dares more will experience more satisfaction.

If you take calculated risks, you get better results and you get better at what you do. This gives you more confidence.

There seems to be a contradiction in this, because risks are full of uncertainty. Still, there is a logic in this apparent contradiction. After all, every time you take risks, you increase your skills. You learn something. This way you build up more self-belief and you are no longer a victim to external circumstances.

The better you get, the more you grow as a human being and the harder you are to replace. That, too, is a form of certainty.

If you have dared to take risks, you can look back at the end of your life and say, *"I did it!"*

In my mind, that is success. Success is not how much money or status you have amassed, but it is: to know what you have done with your life and be satisfied with it.

That is the message I want to send with this book. I hope I can encourage people to jump straight and say, "Yes, now I'm taking action!"

Well?

Are you ready to jump?

Are you ready to jump?

Are you ready to be bold?

For this book, I would like to thank my parents.

'My parents gave me permission to be
who I wanted to be and follow my own path.'

That is the greatest gift to me.
It is priceless.

'To live is the rarest thing in the world.
Most people exist. That is all.'

— Oscar Wilde —